The New Religious Image of Urban America
The Shopping Mall as Ceremonial Center

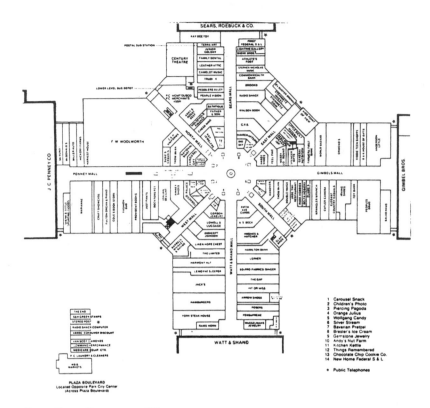

PARK CITY, *Lancaster, PA*

This mall reflects the many circles of a rose window, the quadrilateral design of a mandala, and the floor plan of typical cathedral or basilica. The center in this mall is inescapable.

The New Religious Image of Urban America

The Shopping Mall as Ceremonial Center

SECOND EDITION

IRA G. ZEPP, JR.

with a Foreword and Introduction
by
David Carrasco

University Press of Colorado

© 1997 by the University Press of Colorado
© 1986 by the University Press of Colorado

Published by the University Press of Colorado
P. O. Box 849
Niwot, Colorado 80544
Tel. (303) 530-5337

First edition published in 1986 by Christian Classics, Inc., Westminster, MD.

The University Press of Colorado is a cooperative publishing enterprise supported, in part, by Adams State College, Colorado State University, Fort Lewis College, Mesa State College, Metropolitan State College of Denver, University of Colorado, University of Northern Colorado, University of Southern Colorado, and Western State College of Colorado.

Library of Congress Cataloging-in-Publication Data

Zepp, Ira G.
   The new religious image of urban America : the shopping mall as
ceremonial center / Ira G. Zepp, Jr. ; with a foreword and
introduction by David Carrasco. — 2nd ed.
      p. cm.
   Includes bibliographical references and index.
   ISBN 0-87081-436-2 (pbk. : alk. paper)
   1. Shopping malls—Religious spects. 2. Shopping malls—United
States. 3. United States—Religion—1960– I. Title.
BL2525.Z47 1997
291.3'5—dc21   96-51780
                                      CIP

10 9 8 7 6 5 4 3 2 1

To my mother, father, sisters, and brothers
in gratitude for their love
and for sharing
Saturday night in Bel Air with me.

Contents

Foreword

In my introduction to Ira Zepp's earlier edition of this book, I claimed that he had taken a risk in claiming that a religious world (the Enclosed Mall Air Conditioned Centers (EMACs)) was camouflaged by 20th-century technology. I also indicated that the book would spark considerable debate about the religious dimensions of the malling of America. In fact, Zepp's risk proved to be a wise one, as the book was read from coast to coast and a widespread debate took place in both the academic and popular press. Review comments poured in from the *L.A. Times Mirror*, the *Statesman-Journal* (Salem, Oregon), *The Christian Century*, the *Journal of the History of Religions*, *The World and I*, *The National Catholic Reporter*, and many more.

Some reviewers were rattled by Zepp's insights, as, for instance, "If there is something slightly pathetic and even horrifying about the notion of the shopping mall as the spiritual center of American life, Zepp is too reticent — or too compassionate — to say so." Some were pious, as in, "If he had bothered to . . . probe the depth of the . . . motivations of the average mall developer . . . Zepp would have discovered the quantitative difference, noted by most, between approaching a shopping mall and approaching the Lord"! Still another reviewer gave Zepp the special kudo that he had written a book that would change our perspective on the phenomenon of malls, as in, "You'll never look at mall domes, fountains, skylights and events the same after reading Zepp." Another writer deepened the claim with, "A profound and refreshing work that allows us to see a commonplace of contemporary life in an utterly unexpected way."

So I invite you all to enter into this expanded edition, which shows Zepp both firmer and wiser in his comparison between traditional ceremonial centers and EMACs, but now also airports and ballparks! There is indeed a fresh and important perspective revealed in the second edition of *The New Religious Image of Urban America: The Shopping Mall as Ceremonial Center.* I could do no better than end by quoting what the distinguished urban ecologist and chair of the Committee on Social Thought at the University of Chicago wrote to me after reading the first edition: "Did you put Ira Zepp up to writing about the shopping mall as a ceremonial center? If so, it's about the best thing you could have done. He has treated the malling of America in a way that would simply not have occurred to any of the professional urbanists who plan such complexes — rather as if an ornithologist had thrown entirely new light on the sparrow instead of studying some exotic denizen of the Amazon." In fact, I didn't put Ira Zepp up to it. He put me up to studying sacred space years ago and continues to share new light with those who read him.

DAVÍD CARRASCO
Princeton University
Spring 1996

Preface 1997

Shopping malls are not static institutions. Their dynamism is reflected in how they have transformed and modified themselves over the past decade in adapting to changing consumer needs and desires. If anything, malls are increasingly "more than marketplaces," what with the greater prominence they now give to entertainment facilities and the current importance they attach to providing a multiplicity of human services. Furthermore, the recent trend of malls to providing educational opportunities for all ages, especially young people, is additional evidence of the "more than."

That shopping malls could be viewed as an expression of the human impulse to be religious came across with all the force of novelty, if not skepticism, to many of the readers of the first edition. To just as many, however, there was concurrence with the observation that malls exemplify how people continue to seek community, construct centered spaces, and ritualize their lives. Thus, the assumption: malls are the new icons of urban America and our popular culture.

I have decided to let the 1986 edition be reprinted intact. If the first edition is a kind of period piece, in that some of the data about a few malls are out of date, my underlying thesis and essential argument remain the same. It is still the malls' "mythic geometry" (Eliade), their "architectural rhetoric" (Wheatley), plus the meaningful variety of human activities that take place there, that convince me malls are ceremonial centers as well as places for commercial transactions. For these reasons the new chapter, which updates and rethinks some issues about malls, is entitled "The Mall Is Not Over."

I appreciate the critical analysis the first edition received from thoughtful and careful readers. The concluding chapter benefits greatly from these comments.

I.G.Z.

Preface to the First Edition

The contemporary shopping mall is an heir to the rich legacy of ancient bazaars found on every continent. In 1971, my family visited Mexico, home of one of the world's largest shopping centers. Ten years ago I strolled through a very old, expansive, almost completely covered bazaar in Sarajevo, Yugoslavia. In the summer of 1984, my wife and I traveled in the Middle East and saw bazaars in Jerusalem and Cairo. These were certainly the original festival marketplaces and the models for contemporary American malls. And although they provided an historical and cross-cultural perspective and informed my understanding, in this book I have concentrated on America's malls.

If there appear to be a disproportionate number of references to James Rouse in this study, it is because no one else has reflected more on the nature of malls and marketplaces as human centers. While Rouse's company is not the biggest developer of malls, he is by far the most creative, innovative, and articulate of mall designers. I am grateful to Scott Ditch and Steve Pospisil of the Rouse Company and to Nancy Allison of The Enterprise Development Corporation for their cooperation in providing helpful information and photographs.

The fetal heartbeat of this study began in the academic year 1979–80 when several students in my course, Introduction to Religious Studies, worked with me to discover the religious significance of shopping malls.

The skeletal outline of the book appeared in one of my religion columns in the local *Carroll County Times*. John McHale, editor of Christian Classics, read the column and saw the possibility of a book. For his insight, guidance, support, and patience, I am deeply grateful.

The Research and Creativity Committee and the Philosophy and Religious Studies department of Western Maryland College helped provide funds for research and travel. I have visited more than forty malls in fifteen states.

Mall marketing personnel were — with few exceptions — helpful and interested in the project. Some deserve particular mention: Rebecca Bresson of Fox Hills Mall in Culver City, California, Robert W. Magel, Jr. of Park City, Lancaster, Pennsylvania, Jean E. Redmond, Crossroads Mall, Boulder, Colorado, and Renee Barrett of Lenox Square, Atlanta, Georgia. Donald B. Sutherland of Strawberry Square in Harrisburg, Pennsylvania, and Brian Ulione of White Marsh Mall near Baltimore were very cooperative also.

I also want to thank a few friends who hosted my visits to several cities: Elizabeth and Morris Winkelman in St. Petersburg, Florida, Cindy and Ted Runyon in Atlanta, Georgia, Georgina and Elias Rivers in Stony Brook, New York, Ginny and Harry Wells in Danbury, Connecticut, and Sabrina Bennett in Dallas, Texas.

Virginia Story, our departmental secretary, typed several drafts of the manuscript. This book could not have been completed without her and I greatly appreciate her efficiency and commitment. Beverly McCabe helped with research at the outset of the project and Virginia Gent assisted with typing as the manuscript neared completion. I am especially indebted to Dorothy Shindle who was kind enough to type the final draft.

I owe a debt of gratitude to Gerald Fischman and Ann Henderson who read the manuscript and made very important suggestions concerning grammar and style. They made my somewhat Teutonic sentences much more readable.

A very special word of appreciation is extended to David Carrasco for his gracious and informative introduction.

Most husband-authors pay tribute to their wives for their patience and encouragement. Mary, my wife, has traveled with me to many malls, made valuable criticisms, and been most supportive throughout this study. She also was the final proofreader. So, in Mary's case, the tribute is gladly paid and more than justified. There are no words, only hugs.

I.G.Z.

Acknowledgements

Grateful acknowledgement is made to the following persons for permission to reproduce pictures, schedules, calendars, etc.

Lajuana Grimmett
  Marketing Director
  Nordstrom Mall, Salem, Oregon

Penelope M. Heath
  Marketing Assistant
  Lenox Square
  Atlanta, Georgia

Marilynn Evert
  Adverstising/Marketing Manager
  Tampa Bay Center
  Tampa, Florida

Jan Kline
  Marketing Director
  Gwinnett Place
  Duluth, Georgia

Robert Magell, Jr.
  Marketing Director
  Park City, Lancaster, Pennsylvania

Joan McGuire-Goldberg
  Marketing /Promotion Director
  White Fint
  North Bethesda, Maryland

Leslie B. Schwabe
    Marketing Manager
    White Marsh
    Baltimore, Maryland

Nancy Montgomery
    Washington Cathedral
    Washington, D.C.

Painton Cowen
    London, England

Steve Pospisil
    The Rouse Company
    Columbia, Maryland

Abe Zitren
    Smith Haven Mall
    Lake Grove, N.Y.

Adrianne Frei
    Pendor Natural Color
    Pearl River, New York

Jo Boyster
    Marketing Director
    Crossroads Mall
    Boulder, Colorado

"It's a night on the town. And a day to remember. It's quiet restaurants and theaters. And over 135 exceptional shops and stores. It's fashion. And it's fashionable. It's art shows, flower gardens and pecan reindeer. It's fountains that babble and people that sing. It's the most interesting place ever to get a haircut, mail a letter or service your car. It's monumental sculpture and ample parking. It's in the best location ever. It's Northpark. It's the ultimate. It's the legend. And it's the first place to be for the very last word in shopping."

Promotional brochure for: Northpark Mall
Dallas, Texas

"Let us, however, note one thing which is of importance to our view; to the degree that the ancient holy places, temples or altars lose their religious efficacy, people discover and apply other geomantic, architectural or iconographic formulas which, in the end, sometimes astonishingly enough, represent the same symbolism of the 'Centre.'"

Mircea Eliade
Professor of History of
Religions Emeritus
University of Chicago

"Perhaps each generation creates a kind of mythic building type for itself. What the skyscrapers were to New York in the '30s, the market is today . . . the place where the god of the city has taken up residence for the moment, the place where you take the visiting cousins, the place where, mysteriously, for a time, the Delphic air vibrates."

Robert Campbell
Architectural critic for
the *Boston Globe*

The New Religious Image of Urban America
The Shopping Mall as Ceremonial Center

Introduction

Mircea Eliade, the distinguished historian of religions, wrote in the opening chapter of *Patterns in Comparative Religions*:

> We must get used to the idea of recognizing hierophanies absolutely everywhere, in every area of psychological, economic, spiritual and social life. Indeed we cannot be sure that there is anything — object, movement, psychological function, being or even game — that has not at some time in human history been somewhere transformed into a hierophany . . . it is quite certain that anything man has ever handled, felt, come in contact with or loved can become a hierophany. . . . We know, for instance, that all the gestures, dances and games children have, and many of their toys, have a religious origin — they were once the gestures and objects of worship. In the same way musical and architectural instruments, means of transportation, (animals, chariots, boats, and so on) started by being sacred objects, sacred activities. . . . In the same way too, every trade, art, industry and technical skill either began as something holy, or has, over the years, been invested with religious values. This list could be carried to include man's everyday movement (getting up, walking, running), his various employments (hunting, fishing, agriculture), all his physiological activities (nutrition, sexual life, etc.). (pp. 11–12)

These observations appear in a chapter entitled "Approximations: The Structure and Morphology of the Sacred" which lays out some general patterns by which human actions and natural objects are transformed into "hierophanties" or manifestations of the sacred. As the quote reveals, the history of religions teaches us that *anything* can become sacred or at least be imbued with sacrality.

The present book, written by Ira Zepp, a theologian and phenomenologist of religions, explores the different ways in which those large, massive, labyrinthine, commercial, architectural and festival places called malls appear to be organized spatially by cosmological principles and serve as containers for a number of objects and actions imbued with sacrality. In a real sense, Zepp's book is an "approximation" of the sacred morphology of malls which contain a multiplicity of hierophanies and religious structures. It can be said that Zepp has taken up Eliade's dare; if anything man touches, walks on, builds or plays with can become sacred, then why not EMACs (Enclosed Malls Air Conditioned), especially when they are organized by principles of quadrapartition, operate on festival, calendrical time and are full of symbolic objects?

In Zepp's engaging interpretation, malls, like the objects of Eliade's landscape, are "more," much more than what they appear or even claim to be. As Zepp clearly states, the malls are basically economic centers, compact worlds of capitalism in America. As one other study, *The Malling of America*, has suggested, America has become a Mall. From Zepp's perspective, the moreness of malls, or rather the "otherness" of malls resides in their similarity to the religious, ceremonial centers of traditional civilizations of the ancient world which have recently attracted the careful and continued attention of historians of religions and urban geographers.

In general terms, Zepp's work on the ceremonial order of malls is about a twentieth-century pattern of human, symbolic "orientation" in America. Zepp's pedestrian research (he has literally walked hundreds of miles through American malls as well as exhausted the literature) has revealed the ubiquitous nature of shopping malls in the United States. Communities, large and small, and within their various quarters and sections, are being reorganized around or in relation to various types of shopping malls. Statistical studies of mall-goers have revealed that they spend their largest amount of time (after home and job) in malls. This national trend of commercial and community orientation is a profound but little understood development of American social, commercial, and symbolic life. Zepp's basic question about the magnetic quality and pervasive nature of malls is: "What is the cultural and religious significance of this pattern of social and symbolic orientation?" His strategy to deal with this question is to combine his previously established sensitivity to theological elements in American life with his more recent studies in the hermeneutics and phenomenology of religions and the discoveries of urban geography and ecology. At the center of his eclectic approach are two principles of human orientation found in the spatial and ritual worlds of malls, i.e., the principle of the "symbolism of the center" which is an expression of *homo religiosus*, and the principle of ritual regeneration which is an expression of *homo ludens*, the human as player. This complex mode of orientation combining reverence for a center-oriented world with the human need for play and regeneration is, according to Zepp, imprinted on the physiognomy, scheduling, and activities of malls. As his remarkable chapter on the entrepreneur-Christian-founder of malls, James Rouse, demonstrates, the planning of some of the malls included cosmological and soteriological purposes from the beginning.

Zepp has taken a risk in turning his religious studies scholarship onto the complexities of malls. His work is the first to raise the question of cultural and symbolic patterns and meanings in these great roadside attractions. As the reader will discover, Zepp's heartfelt reflections on places such as Lenox Square, Park City, Fox Hills, White Marsh, and Galleria come in three voices. While he is constantly striving to gain an interpretive edge on the phenomena of malls, he is also painting a world of hope and finally expressing a lament for a bygone geography of human community. In order to understand the complex crossings of Zepp's three voices, a few words about his interpretive approach will prove helpful. Whether the reader agrees with his perspective or not, one will learn a great deal about this pattern in American culture as well as gain a positive interpretive stance from which to think about EMACs.

Some of the theoretical background for Zepp's approach is derived from Mircea Eliade's conception of the "Symbolism of the Center" and Paul Wheatley's study of "ideal-type ceremonial centers" in traditional cities.[1] Both scholars emphasize the human tendency to organize all modes of human life around ceremonial centers which derive their authority from celestial archetypes that are replicated in cultural conceptions of space and time. In Eliade's broad comparative studies, "reality is conferred through participation in the symbolism of the Center: cities, temples, houses become real by the fact of being assimilated to the 'center of the world.'" In the history of religions, human beings organize their lives around sacred centers such as mountains, temples, cities, and ceremonial precincts which acquire the prestige of being an *axis mundi*, the axis of the world which joins supernatural and human forces together. These sacred centers, found everywhere in human history, serve to orient not only symbolic maps in a society, but also architecture, mental constructs, patterns of economic exchange, ritual pilgrimages and conceptions of the soul.

Paul Wheatley utilized a number of Eliade's discoveries in his study of the origins and character of pristine urban societies in the seven areas of primary urban generation. Wheatley discovered that in Egypt, Mesopotamia, China, the Indus Valley, Africa, Mesoamerica and Peru, that is, where cities were invented independently, a threefold symbolism which he calls "cosmo-magical" thought served to organize the so-

1. See Mircea Eliade, *The Myth of the Eternal Return* (New York: Pantheon Books, 1965); Eliade, *Patterns In Comparative Religions* (New York: Meridian Books, 1967), and Paul Wheatley, *The Pivot of the Four Quarters* (Chicago: Aldine Press, 1971), for elaborate discussions of the model which Zepp is utilizing.

cial and ecological complexities of society. Besides the a) ever present and powerful symbolism of the center, Wheatley identified b) the pattern of dividing ceremonial precincts into four quarters which surrounded a central ceremonial precinct. This pattern of cardinal axiality was often highlighted by c) the practice of symbolic parallelism in which certain buildings or ritual precincts were dramatic images in stone of cosmogonic myths or dramatic celestial archetypes. These "brick thoughts" were architecturally constructed to dramatize the connections between celestial influence and human life. What is interesting for Zepp's study is that both Eliade and Wheatley were impressed by the world-wide tendency of ancient urban dwellers to organize their worlds on the basis of cosmological models dramatized in ceremonial centers.

Some of the big questions that must be asked of Zepp's work are, has he accurately gauged the similarity between the symbolic patterns of traditional ceremonial centers and the contemporary shopping malls? Has he, in fact, uncovered the remnants of a *discarded* model of spatial organization which are surprisingly coherent in these grandiose centers of exchange? Has he clearly seen a religious world camouflaged by twentieth-century technology? Can we see what he sees?

We see Zepp's exploration of this ancient/contemporary parallelism in sections entitled "Cosmic Tree," "Symbols of the Center," "Water of Life," "Festival Marketplace," and in chapters on sacred space and time. One of the most convincing arguments for the religious character of malls appears in his startling chapter, "James Rouse, Mahatma of Malls." We discover that the vision, financial activities, and plans of Rouse are illuminated through Zepp's use of the idea of a religious "founder." If the scholar of religion and psychology, Peter Homans, is correct that "origins cue structure," then the structure of many American malls is decisively religious because the founder of the finest malls in America had an elaborate religious purpose in building them in the first place. It is surprising to learn just how intertwined the notions of city, festival, sacred space, cosmological parallelism and religious values were in James Rouse's life and mall dreams. For Rouse, malls were part of the co-creativity of God and people in America. This chapter alone gives truth to Zepp's claim that religious symbolism and values are imprinted on the history and character of American malls.

This interpretation is framed in the book by chapters of nostalgia and lament. In the opening chapter, "Saturday Night in Bel Air," Zepp reveals that he had something like a religious experience growing up in Maryland, especially on those Saturday nights when he traveled the long, winding road from his family's isolated farm house to go "uptown" to the town of Bel Air. This periodic journey opened up new feelings of human community and created a long-lasting sense of orientation in his world. As he recalls the space, the characters and feelings of human connection, we see the ghosts of humorous, decent, frail human beings who, like the unique characters of *Winesburg, Ohio*, have been left behind by the establishment of new centers of American life. In the book's final chapter, "From Lenox Square to Bel Air," Zepp faces squarely the limits and disappointments of this massive shift to the great shopping malls.

Zepp's readable, humane interpretation of the worlds of Bel Air and Lenox Square is a special act of understanding. He has raised some important human questions in an optimistic, intriguing way.

DAVÍD CARRASCO

• 1 •

More than a Marketplace: The Religious Nature of Shopping Malls

What is Religious About Malls?

"Do you teach business?" asked one mall manager when I told him I was writing a book on shopping malls. On another occasion, a marketing specialist for malls asked, "Do you teach geography?" This specialist was more imaginative, but the truth is that I teach religious studies. And when I first mentioned to people, either socially or while interviewing them, that I was writing a book on the religious dimensions of shopping malls, there were usually two responses.

The first was cynical laughter, followed by "You've got to be kidding," or "Now, I've heard everything."

The other type of reaction — and this was by far more frequent — ranged from curiosity to enthusiasm to fascination. These people would often say, "I know just the mall you should see" or "There is this neat mall I recommend." It was as if each person had his or her own special mall, felt emotionally attached to it, and thought it indispensable for my research.

And quite apart from the laughter and suspicion of the first group, both responses indicate just how much the shopping mall has engraved itself on our consciousness. One thing was certain — no one yawned and asked "What else is new?" when I mentioned this project.

There is hardly a major community in the United States which has not built a shopping mall or expects to construct one soon. For better or worse, the shopping mall is part of our language, mythology, everyday life, and culture. It will not quickly disappear. On the contrary, it is one of the fastest growing commercial phenomena in the country. In fact, as long ago as 1971, S. Buddy Harris of Gruen Associates said, "Our mall planning is for the year 2000."

One observer, Bill Thomas of Baltimore's *The Sunday Sun*, wrote that malls "have become so much a part of the everyday landscape that it's as hard to imagine an America without malls as it is to imagine an America without purple mountains and amber waves of grain."[1]

Twelve years ago, *U.S. News and World Report*, a journal which has followed closely the growth of malls, said, "Next to time spent on the job and at home, more and more Americans are spending the largest part of their time at the malls."[2] And in the last decade, mall mania has increased even more.

The mall is the new village square, encompassing all the social and economic forces associated with that expression of human community. All of this "malling" has not gone unnoticed. Charles Kuralt of CBS created an interesting television special on malls. Most business and news magazines have devoted articles to the growth of these commercial establishments. Indeed, you can find more than two dozen relevant articles in the *Reader's Guide to Periodical Literature* over the last decade.

Observers, reporters, and journalists describe the malls rather unimaginatively. They frequently remark off-handedly on how malls are replete with trees and fountains, as if such things were placed there fortuitously. They wonder why people are fascinated with malls and much of their commentary is skewed toward the business side of things.

One pleasant exception is William S. Kowinski's fine study in *New Times*, "The Malling of America." * I have borrowed his title for part 2 of Chapter 2. While critical of malls, he perceives them as a place which fulfills many levels of human need. However I believe he lacks a basic appreciation of their cultural and religious significance.

To date, no systematic analysis of the mall has been attempted from a religious studies perspective. It is my contention that phenomenology of religion and history of religion offer us the most illuminating hermeneutical lens through which we can see — at a deeper, more human level — the meaning and magnetism of the mall. Using the interpretive framework of religion, we can gain more insight into our attraction to these festival marketplaces. So my concern is not that of a business analyst or marketing specialist, but that of a student of religion, a field in which myth, symbol, and ritual are taken seriously as human expressions.

As I have mentioned, there is a good deal of cynicism about viewing malls positively. Many people see malls only as places designed for profit — "A mall is a mall." Their criticisms are found in comments such as: "Face it, malls are there to make money and everything they do has a dollar sign in front of it" or "It is a capitalist rip-off dressed up in a tuxedo or circus tent."

I don't minimize the commercial nature of these shopping centers. After all, they consist predominantly of stores and eating places where goods and services are bought and sold. Promotional and social events in the mall, however philanthropic they may appear, will not continue if they eventually

---

*While this book was being completed, Kowinski's article appeared in book form by the same title. *The Malling of America*, New York: William Morrow and Co., 1985.

do not produce a profit. As one mall manager told me, "We are not primarily a public service. Our direct intention is to attract customers."

While I don't deny the truth in all these statements, I submit that malls as we experience them cannot be reduced to commercial and financial enterprises. They are far more than places of business. I want to take the malling of America seriously as a popular cultural movement reflecting religious elements as old as the human race. Malls are as multi-faceted and complex as you would expect a typical social institution to be.

Once inside a mall, shoppers are often overwhelmed by its sheer size, its many colors and sounds, and the constant activity. Yet, people feel ambivalent about their attraction to them. Emotional and intellectual access to this rapidly growing and remarkable phenomenon might be easier by way of this religious interpretation.

First of all, from the point of view of the religious person (homo religiosus), the mall represents an "ontological thirst for orientation" (Mircea Eliade). This theme is elaborated at length in the chapters on the mall as sacred center and secular cathedral. The desire for orientation may be one way to understand our enchantment with malls. We long for bearings beyond the utilitarian, the pragmatic, and the monotonous — an unconscious, yet pervasive yearning of the contemporary person.

Secondly, listen to how some malls describe themselves: "We are more than a shopping center," "We are much more than a marketplace," "We are more than a collection of shops." It is this "much more than" that interests me and which triggered this study. This "much more than," whether realized consciously or not, is a religious reference, maybe even a metaphysical one, and provides the real mystique of the malls.

I must confess that initially I was genuinely surprised at

this self-description by the malls. It was unexpected and I was compelled by my curiosity to do some intellectual sleuthing to probe the accuracy of this description.

By participating in this journey, you may see if the ancient holy places which have lost their religious efficacy might be, astonishingly enough, represented by contemporary malls. If the mall is, as I am contending, a "camouflage of the sacred," then the "more than" of the malls' publicity brochures has a rich symbolic structure worth examining. We will see that the "more than" refers to several things.

First, the mall is concurrently a centered world and a place of festival. Both these elements constitute some fundamental aspects of a ceremonial center. A mall is such a center because of its design and as a result of what takes place there. Its construction and ritual activity betray its ceremonial nature.

Secondly, the average mall contains natural and social forces. The union of energy provided by vegetation, water, and people tends to diffuse the tension we all experience between the technical and pastoral, the urban and the rural, or as literary historian Leo Marx says, "the machine and the garden."

And thirdly, the average mall's "architectural rhetoric" (a phrase urban geographer Paul Wheatley applies to sacred centers) betrays its involvement in something beyond business transactions. Some malls, such as the Galleria in White Plains, New York and White Marsh in Maryland, appear from the outside a mixture of cathedral and castle. And many, among them Smith Haven on Long Island and Lenox Square in Atlanta, have an excessively decorative and ornate quality about their interior space.

It is this "more than" which gives the mall its religious character. I hasten to add that when the word "religion" is used in this book, it is not to be identified with denominational affiliation, adherence to belief, the practice of a certain religious institution (church or synagogue), or faith in a supreme being. I do not wish to deprecate the popular notion and practice of religion; rather I am suggesting a more expansive view that permits us to see how religion is a dimension of human experience.

This definition of religion transcends the normal understanding. I am concerned with the religious person — *homo religiosus* — the tendency of human beings to re-link, re-bind, re-connect, and re-concile themselves with each other and nature. This is precisely what the Latin *re-ligare* (from which the English word "religion" is derived) means. Whenever people are in the process of restoring life to wholeness, integration and unity, they are engaging in religious activity.

Specifically for my purposes here, the impulse of people to symbolize their lives and of human communities to revitalize their lives are inescapable aspects of the human venture. All human activity includes symbols, and malls are no exception.

If someone thinks I am making more out of malls than is really there, my response is simply that what people do is more important than what they say, or rather, what we do is a way of speaking. So however we disclaim the transcommercial nature of malls, the fact we are going to them in droves deserves investigation and analysis.

When something has imposed itself on our personal consciousness and social fabric with as much force as the malls, it is worthy of attention by culture watchers and academics. It is the magnetic quality and pervasive nature of the malls that I want to examine. Furthermore, this is not an attempt to force malls into preconceived types or to make them fit certain religious patterns. On the contrary, when one is familiar with religious motifs, themes, and symbols, and lets the mall "speak," the conclusion seems obvious.

Much less am I a messiah for malls. Certainly malls present a great many limitations as a human "world," precisely at the point of their self-designated strength. This will be discussed in the final chapter.

Finally, I am not assuming that much of what is said in this book reflects the conscious intentions or motivations of the average mall developer, architect, clerk, or customer. As someone once said, only a flying fish discovers water. And so, an outside observer — someone with detachment — might discover that the mall is more than a marketplace. It is interchangeably and simultaneously a ceremonial center, an alternative community, a carnival, and a secular cathedral.

My two major themes will be the human propensity to symbolize and ritualize life, *homo religiosus*, especially in centers and communities and the person at play, *homo ludens*, the human propensity to engage in festival.

Mircea Eliade, internationally respected historian of religions, observed that many human acts do not arise from pure automatism. "Their meaning, their value, are not connected with their crude physical datum but with their property of reproducing a primordial act, of repeating a mythical example."[3]

In this book, I will try to answer the questions: What primordial act is being reproduced by the ever-increasing number of shopping malls? To what reality do these malls point? What resonates in us making us find them so attractive and fascinating? What meanings are we deriving from their symbolic and ritual structure? What is the "more than" of shopping malls?

· 2 ·

From Bel Air to Lenox Square

Saturday Night in Bel Air

Thirty-five years ago, Saturday night was the most crowded and easily the most memorable time of the week in my hometown. All roads led to this small rural community, the county seat of Harford County, Maryland. On Saturday night, extra police were hired to direct traffic at the intersection of Main and Office Streets. There was no traffic light in those days. The influx of people and automobiles made this part of town a literal and figurative center of activity.

People came here on Saturday night, ostensibly to shop. Most of them no doubt had a business reason for being in town. But a lot more than commercial transactions was taking place in Bel Air on that night.

"Going uptown," my father used to call it. "I'm going to see what's happening uptown." The spatial reference "up" had nothing to do with topography or terrain. It was a relatively flat area. "Up" had, apparently, a qualitative reference; it had to do with a different sort of space.

"Uptown" as a metaphor was invariably relegated to Saturday night, when all the stores were open until 9 or 10 P.M. "Uptown" as a geographical space was a two-block-long business district along Main Street.

The possibilities for shopping seemed endless. There were

two barber shops, an ice cream store, two restaurants, two drug stores, three clothing establishments, one shoe store, a florist, an optician, a stationery store, a Woolworth's five-and-dime, a fruit market, two home appliance stores, a furniture store, a luncheon/deli, a tavern, a discount store, a shoe repair shop, an auto appliance shop, a jewelry store, an old hotel, a movie theater, a bank, a jail, and a courthouse. The business district was bound on one end by a car dealership and on the other by a National Guard Armory. All in all, it was not an unusual collection of shops and stores for an American small town in the 1940s.

The "park" was the heart and center of this shopping district. Not a park in the usual sense of the word, this was a small area between the jail lawn and the sidewalk on Main Street. In this space, approximately seventy-five feet long and ten feet wide, stood about six wooden, green-slatted benches under some large, stately trees. The courthouse with its shade trees and fountain filled with flowers was directly across the street from the park.

Very close to the park and on the same side of the street, in front of Preston's Stationery Store, were two stairways — one which led down to the poolroom and bar and the other to a barbershop. Since the stairs descended horizontally along the sidewalk, two sturdy brass rails were added to prevent people from falling into the stairwells. On Saturday night, men — I never saw women there — would gather to lean against these rails and socialize.

These special spots would attract the same men each Saturday night. (The park benches were occupied occasionally by women.) On the rails or the benches they would catch up with the week's gossip, watch women go by, see who got off the bus from Baltimore (which stopped right next to the park), argue politics, spin some grass roots philosophy, reminisce about the good old days, and discuss sports. The International League Baltimore Orioles (the NFL Colts did not exist then), the local semi-pro Susquehanna baseball league (which eventually produced the Orioles' Dick Hall and Cal Ripken, Sr.), and the hottest athletic activity in post-World War II Bel Air — night softball — were all welcome topics of conversation. Softball was played by a league of rather competent amateur teams sponsored by local businesses and for a few years the league was the talk of the town. Mind you, this was before television was a household item.

"What's the scoop?" was a greeting often heard when these men met one another. They were mostly blue-collar workers, intensely hard-working and loyal Americans, for whom going "uptown" was the highlight of the week. There was a certain male bonding experienced here, although most of the men would have been perplexed to hear their relationships defined in those terms.

Even though we had a variety of shops on Main Street, there were obviously other reasons for being in Bel Air on Saturday night. Purchasing goods became the catalyst for a community celebration.

For many, Saturday night in Bel Air was primarily a social event, a time when you went "uptown" to "see the sights." It meant meeting people and reconnecting with a group you had not seen for a week or so. Connection was not only reestablished among men who came to the park and the rails. It was also between store clerk and customer, cop and pedestrian, sheriff's deputy (needed mostly for a rowdy drunk or two) and the crowd with whom the law officer mingled freely, school teachers and students (how strange it was for us students to see teachers shopping like ordinary people), and parents and teachers (an impromptu P.T.A. meeting could take place on Main Street). I learned later, in sociology classes, that all of this represented a primary community, a "*Gemeinschaft*," where people have a face-to-face, first-hand knowledge of each other. Personal relationships tended to be the norm here.

Even when purchases were made, there was a personal dimension to the transactions. The manager undoubtedly knew not only the customer but his or her parents and grandparents.

Questions about the health, welfare, and location of Aunt Mary, Uncle Phil or Cousin Betsy were as natural in the conversation as the price of the product or the terms of payment. The blending of the commercial and the human was necessary for the survival of any small-town marketplace.

Bel Air on Saturday night was not a very resourceful place for teenagers. The post-war baby boom had not come of age. There were, naturally, a few teen hangouts — the soda fountain in Woolworth's and the two drugstores. Junior high school-age kids — the teenyboppers of today who frequent malls in such numbers — were not much in evidence. They were either at home with their families or accompanying their parents uptown. The mid- and late teenage kids met on Saturday night, walking uptown with a date or driving to town to see a movie. Very few would come there looking for dates. (In those days that was not "downright upright" for either sex.)

Many young men, away from home for a few hours, mustered the courage to use the blessedly anonymous drug store pay telephones to call their latest crushes for dates. How awesome that was!

Generally, there was an unselfconscious mixing of the generations — the young, the middle-aged, and the elderly. Natural and informal subgroups, usually defined by age and sex, converged on Saturday night.

On that night in Bel Air, a distinct sense of carnival prevailed. You knew instinctively that this was a different time than Wednesday afternoon. You could sense it in the air. Festivity, color, and laughter were all there. Next to wearing your Sunday best for church, dressing up for Saturday night ranked high on the costuming list. A certain buoyancy and levity permeated the scene. It is what we in religious studies call "sacred time" — time apart, discontinuous time, special time, totally different time, a "break." It was "time out" from the ordinariness of the week.

It was not milking time, planting time, harvesting time, or drilling time. On the contrary, it was time to let your hair down, to suspend seriousness, and to escape from the nine-to-five routine of the factory or the unending demands of farm life.

Saturday night in Bel Air was a post-World War II forerunner of Saturday night fever. Saturday night was live in Bel Air. That time was a big deal, the social event of the week. It was part town meeting, part innocence, part carnival, part sexual fantasy, part business, part human renewal, part recreation — all of which describe a religious and ceremonial center. Certainly my hometown was not unique. What I have described was a typical Main Street in small town America during the pre-1950s building boom, an era of population growth.

Some people were indispensable to Saturday night in Bel Air. You would inevitably encounter them that evening along Main Street. These characters helped create the gestalt of that high moment of the week and represented the organic nature of that community which gathered there. Saturday night would have paled if these people were absent — part of the weekend ritual was to see them.

Most likely on that night you would want to purchase a Sunday paper, and that meant a visit to John. John was in his late fifties and had the franchise to sell the Baltimore Sunday papers, whose early editions arrived in Bel Air Saturday evening. The papers were stacked up against the Commercial and Savings Bank. John stood beside them. He wore an apron with pockets, so he could make change easily.

John was there year 'round. If the weather were bad, he would sell papers from his car, parked nearby. Always a small group of people assembled around John. He excelled in details and was considered a kind of human computer. Batting averages of local and national baseball players, the record of the hottest and coldest days, who was related to whom, the size of the most recent funeral — John knew them all. He had a real gift for conversation, was unpretentious, and really liked people.

If you looked away from the bank and onto Main Street, you would no doubt spot Milton. He was about thirty-five years old at that time and had been severely disabled from early childhood. His body language and speech revealed a form of cerebral palsy. He was deputized, given a uniform, and on Saturday night was allowed to direct traffic. This was how the town accepted graciously someone who in other times or places might be ignored or excluded. Milton had a keen mind, a delightful sense of humor, and a sense of responsibility. He loved the honorary status the sheriff's office bestowed on him and was rarely taken for granted. I am amazed, looking back, that the town could so effectively and humanly absorb Milton and invest him with such dignity.

After chatting with John you might find your way to Preston's Stationery store a few yards away. Sooner or later, for one reason or another, almost everyone ended up at Preston's on Saturday night. Stanley Preston owned and managed the store adjacent to the rail. Besides office supplies, he sold magazines, greeting cards, candy, tobacco, and small gift items. Stanley was a kind, firm, no-nonsense, courtly shop keeper. He had a jaunty walk and when he passed you he gave you an affirming pat on the back. His Quaker background instilled a sense of industry, integrity, good business acumen, and utmost fairness.

He was my employer for two years between high school and college and for two summers during my college career. I remember vividly how he helped older and infirm men and women get up and down the steps to his store. Business here was conducted in a friendly and personal atmosphere. Stanley knew almost everyone who patronized the store.

Coming down the steps from Preston's, you would see the rail immediately on your right. There, among other "regulars," as sure as it was Saturday night, would be Ned — a witty, engaging, macho hulk of a man with a barrel chest rounded by powerful arms. Ned's right leg had been amputated just below the hip following a motorcycle accident. The stump would rest in a section of his crutch as he leaned against the rail. It was difficult for Ned to be inconspicuous; his strong and compelling ego demanded the center of attention. And, indeed, people were drawn to him, perhaps because of his disability and the remarkable way he compensated for it. We all received vicarious strength from his presence. He seemed invincible.

Either on the rail or seated in the park you could find George. This tall, professorial peripatetic had strolled uptown from his nearby home. He was a draftsman and a highbrow, who did not find it beneath him to associate with the ordinary folks frequenting the park. George was our resident intellectual and philosophized about the meaning of weather while John would recall the temperature. People kidded about George's "high falutin'" language and nervous energy, but they took him in stride. He did not intimidate them. He meant well, was never demeaning, and, above all, was one of us.

Then, very close to the park, you would hear a loud belly laugh. You knew Joe, the fishmonger, had arrived. He would peddle fish caught in the Chesapeake Bay and the Bush River — only ten to fifteen miles south of town. He was a short, bowlegged, toothless man who dressed in working clothes. His leathery, craggy face reflected years of exposure to the sun and the harsh water. Joe, with that hearty laugh and repertoire of jokes, was our clown and jester. He served an important function and felt very much at home with his buddies on Main Street. Saturday night would not have been the same without him.

Invariably, at some moment that night, Raymond would

walk through the jail's front yard and into the park. He was the ramrod-stiff county sheriff, respected by all. He had the knack of engaging and disengaging when appropriate, of being personal with the crowd which gathered that night in front of the jail and being distant when the men began to exploit his relationship with them. He knew the boundaries and guarded them well. Raymond was deeply conscientious and absolutely fair in law enforcement, a model of decency, and the epitome of what we expected from police officers.

All of these men contributed to the human mosaic that was our community on Saturday night. I mention them because such people provide an aspect of community the mall cannot achieve, even though it tries very hard to be that kind of personal place.

The nature of a small community allows the benefits and richness of such characters to be shared and remembered. These people gave Bel Air a distinction, something personal and earthy, human and unpredictable.

Saturday night in Bel Air was a time and place for goods to be purchased (a commercial center) and for people to interact (a human community). It was more than a business district; it was really a festival center as well. The center fulfilled many of the conscious and unconscious needs of those who came in from the surrounding area.

Times such as Saturday night in Bel Air were the forerunners of the contemporary mall. If you had placed a roof over those two blocks in Bel Air and controlled the climate, you would almost have the contemporary air-conditioned enclosed shopping mall.

Although the mall is a contrived version of Bel Air, which was a more natural human community, it may be all the later twentieth- and early twenty-first centuries can offer. Developer James Rouse wanted desperately to recapture in his shopping centers the kind of community we experienced in Bel Air.

I hasten to add that Bel Air no longer exists as I have described it. Uptown Bel Air has been completely redeveloped; the park and rails are gone. "Saturday night" is no more. A roof was put over that two-block area and moved a mile out of town. It is now the new Harford Mall.

The Malling of America

In a sense, it is a long way geographically and culturally from Bel Air to Lenox Square in Atlanta, Georgia. Lenox Square is ranked by many experts among the top ten malls in the country. For its twentieth anniversary in 1979, Lenox Square published a brochure which stated: "The United States has given three things to the world: jazz, musical comedy, and the shopping center. Let's be honest. If most of us could keep just one of them, it would be the shopping center."

Well, notwithstanding the hype and the doubt that musical comedy and shopping centers originated here (remember Gilbert and Sullivan and Middle Eastern bazaars), this observation does illustrate how seriously malls view themselves and the hold they have on the minds of late-twentieth-century Americans.

Although Victor Gruen Associates, a pioneer firm in mall design, drew up plans for a mall in Forth Worth in 1955, city officials were not enamored by the idea and turned it down. The first example of a mall, as we know it today, was built in Southdale Center, outside of Minneapolis, in 1956. There are now more than 15000 malls of the EMAC (Enclosed Mall Air-Conditioned) variety in existence or in the process of being built. Together they gross approximately 4–5 billion dollars a year.

Malls dot the suburban landscape at pivotal junctions of major highways, usually beltways and interstates, so the broadest base of population has access to them. Some are located in our larger cities' downtown areas, which are served by mass transit. These marketplaces average from 100–200 stores covering hundreds of thousands of square feet. Some of the more recent malls, such as Gwinnett Place outside Atlanta which opened in February 1984, average between one and five million square feet of shopping space.

Over the last fifty years America has witnessed the rapid progression from the general store at the rural crossroads, to the small town square, to the suburban strip shopping center with open-faced stores, to the city pedestrian malls, to the huge regional suburban malls — which are, in fact, miniature commercial cities.

The car-free pedestrian mall, which emerged in the 1960s in urban downtown areas, did not become the success that was anticipated. There were unquestionable drawbacks.

First, there was the complication of having to drive through heavy traffic and then solve the subsequent parking problem with all the attendant expense. Since there were rarely parking facilities at the promenade, traffic congestion kept many shoppers from attempting the drive.

Secondly, the pedestrian mall followed the dictionary definition of a mall — it had only a shaded walkway, which did not include a roof or cover to shelter shoppers from rain, snow, or other inclement weather. Rain-soaked benches had to be wiped off, snow shoveled, and leaves raked. Extra energy and money were expended because of this exposure to the elements. So Lenox Square and many other pedestrian malls made the next logical step. They enclosed the mall and that is the usual pattern — the EMAC today.

There are now several major kinds of EMACs — the type of mall which is my primary, though not exclusive, concern. Although many EMACs call themselves shopping centers, squares, or plazas, when a center is covered, it is a mall as defined here.

The central city mall is often called Gallery; sometimes the original Italian Galleria is used. This is a multi-storied edifice with balconies. Indeed, the word "gallery" refers to a roofed promenade or balcony. The vertical nature of the structure allows the developers to make up in height what they lose in breadth on the ground.

Philadelphia and Houston provide excellent examples of inner city gallerias. In fact, the Houston and Dallas gallerias are modeled after the famous Galleria Vittoria Emanuelle built in Milan, Italy in 1867. These two Texas gallerias are distinguished for their arched glass roofs — replicas of the one in Milan.

The regional mall outside the metropolitan area is invariably dependent on some means of public and private transportation. It can cover hundreds of acres, including parking lots. Typically, there will be four or five major department stores, one at each of the major entrances. These, appropriately enough, are called "anchor stores." At its largest, such a mall can resemble a small town, offering every conceivable service and imaginable sale item.

The newer and even smaller specialty mall, composed solely of small stores and boutiques, appeals to a special clientele. Such malls are intentionally elitist. They have, to be sure, a variety of shops, including restaurants, but no anchor stores. These malls are often next to convention hotels and large office complexes. The Galleria in Atlanta is an example.

The growth of these shopping centers, generically referred to as malls, is a response to three needs of the American consuming public. The three were outlined by James Rouse over twenty years ago.*

1) The enormous internal change in American cities reflected in urban flight, or at least urban sprawl. As downtowns decayed, cities had to reorganize. Often, a key part of

---

*This material is a paraphrase from Rouse's observations in "The Regional Shopping Center: Its Role in the Community It Serves." Lecture at Harvard Graduate School of Design, April 26, 1963.

that revitalization was a multi-storied central city mall—
what we have come to call the Gallery. There are a number
of these—in Houston, Dallas, Philadelphia, and the reno-
vated old city Post Office in Washington, D.C.

In the middle 1970s, cities located on bodies of water began
to develop attractive marketplaces along their waterfronts.
This trend was inspired by James Rouse who built South
Street Seaport in New York City, Waterside in Norfolk, and
Harborplace in Baltimore. City and state officials agree invariably that these festival marketplaces have done "mir-
acles" for community pride and human interaction.

"The South Street Seaport," said Governor Mario Cuomo
of New York, "shows what can be done when government,
business, and labor work together. It is like the Brooklyn
Bridge—part of the past, part of the new, and part of the future." And Mayor Edward Koch of New York City could
hardly contain himself at the dedication of South Street Seaport. "I'm coming down here almost every day for lunch. I invite you all to join me—Dutch Treat."

William Donald Schaefer, mayor of Baltimore, is convinced that his beloved Harborplace is the gem of the city
which has helped prove his prediction of ten years ago. "People will soon spend their vacations in Baltimore."

2) Technology of transportation. Although we are less dependent on public transportation than we once were, the
automobile is ineffecent in cities, given parking problems,
congestion, and pollution.

Since Rouse's speech, most urban areas have developed
very efficient mass transit systems, often including subways.
This has permitted access both to the suburbs and to the inner
city.

3) The drastic change in our shopping habits and, to a
larger degree, our way of life. We do not work from dawn to
dusk anymore and most of us have more time and money.
Families often shop together in the evening. The mall repre-

sents the less formal, more casual style of life which has generally pervaded our culture.

There is another need to which the mall responds – the need to feel safe while shopping. This is implied in another of Rouse's statements: "We need to replace the image of a ragged, low income, unsafe street with the expectancy of a festival marketplace."

In short, the mall is perceived as a serene, crime-free area. As one elderly shopper said to me in St. Petersburg, Florida, "My wife and I feel safe in here. There is no mugging here, you know." Some regional malls even pride themselves on being located out of reach of an urban transit system. Of course, this is code language for being free of the poor, the riff-raff, and other undesirables.

This last point requires us to acknowledge another element in the malling of America. You find a certain elitism while surveying the gamut of malls.

Most malls, admittedly, appeal to a middle-class, egalitarian-oriented public. The anchor stores represented by such chains as Sears, J. C. Penney, and Montgomery Ward symbolize the middle-brow taste. Although there may be one or two relatively fancy restaurants in these average malls, most have a food court composed of fast-food outlets. These malls strive to be all things to all people. Dress is casual and entertainment is geared for the average consumer. There are, however, some significant examples of overlap between middle- and upper-class expression in malls. For example, in Dallas' Prestonwood Mall you find Nieman-Marcus and Lord and Taylor along with J. C. Penney and Montgomery Ward.

The upper-class malls — much fewer in number — will have small specialty shops or prestigious anchor stores such as Lord and Taylor, Saks Fifth Avenue, and Nieman-Marcus. Most of these malls' developers would not consider having a fast food court or such exhibits as boat shows and flea markets. And you certainly would not find an ear-piercing booth at the entrance. These malls want to attract select customers who know what they want. People go there to buy, rarely to shop. An example: Phipps Plaza in Atlanta. It is relatively small (little more than sixty stores), squeaky clean, and well-appointed to reflect its fashion-conscious clientele. The shops have few clever names; they attempt to convey taste and sophistication, e.g., The Executive Image in women's wear, Godiva Chocolatier in the food department, Classic Crystal in gifts and novelties, and Dean Witter Reynolds, Inc. in the area of services.

The presence of Saks Fifth Avenue, Lord and Taylor, Tiffany and Company, Gucci, and Abercrombie and Fitch give you the air of New York's Fifth Avenue. There are no Sears and Wards here! Phipps Plaza bills itself as a place "hand-selected to satisfy the discriminating shopper."

In these malls you find little "hanging out" by young or old. There are fewer benches and less public space provided at the center for social gathering. The malls with such appeal and self-conscious exclusiveness know their clientele. The customers come with something on their mind, go to a shop, make their purchase, and usually leave.

Not infrequently, this type of mall attracts the local landed gentry as well as the well-to-do tourist staying in a nearby hotel or attending a conference. This mall also survives because of its ability to lure the upwardly mobile who benefit vicariously from the posh image and bourgeois nature of these elite meeting places.

While recognizing some classism in the malling of our society, the American shopping mall generally is a middle class institution. It is America in miniature. As one clerk in Atlanta said, "Here in Lenox Square you have a hot dog stand and Nieman-Marcus. On Saturdays everyone comes — from bag ladies to punk rockers to wealthy matrons."

With few exceptions, the shopping mall reflects the American disdain for elitism and exclusivity. The egalitarian streak, which runs so deeply in the American spirit, is evident in the openness and inclusiveness of most malls. As James Rouse says, "Shopping is the most democratic of all experiences. It includes everyone, and a central city marketplace is the most democratic institution in the city."

On a later occasion, Rouse said, as if to emphasize the point, "It is in the marketplace that all people come together — rich and poor, old and young, black and white. It is the democratic, unifying, universal place which gives spirit and personality to the city. . . ." Scott Ditch, Rouse's colleague, reinforces the contention that malls have the broadest possible appeal by claiming: "We go for the middle of the market."

From an ecclesiastical point of view, the average mall, with its democratic appeal, resembles a Catholic church at worship more than a Protestant one. Since Catholics are expected to attend their parish church, you can often find a millionaire kneeling beside a laborer. The hierarchy of economic classes in the parish are leveled once a person is in the church.

Protestant denominations tend to reflect that hierarchy and a class consciousness. H. Richard Niebuhr, Yale theologian of a generation ago, wrote about the "social sources of Protestant denominationalism." He noticed that there were high-class, middle-class, and low-class churches in Protestantism. It is interesting that malls, in general, have avoided this social stratification. Ironically enough, a Protestant, James Rouse, envisioned malls as egalitarian, with a "catholic," universal appeal.

Convenience is the obvious advantage of the mall for the consumer. One-stop shopping is the "come on" we often hear. Almost anything you want and most of what you need can be found here — from an evening gown to a water bed to a guitar to a taco to an automobile tune-up to a filling for one's teeth to counseling for a family problem.

White Marsh Mall in Maryland lists in its promotional brochure the following services available under one roof: department stores, financial services, home fashions and furnishings, books and stationery, fast food restaurants, fashion apparel, jewelry and gifts, personal care and service, specialty shops, home entertainment, shoes, sports and leisure, and photography and camera supplies.

I asked a twenty-year-old man in an Atlanta mall parking lot why he frequented a particular mall. His reply was immediate. "You come here and get everything. You can entertain yourself. You can feed yourself and you can shop if you want to." In precisely that order, he responded very quickly. "Convenience plus entertainment" is the phrase often used by mall promoters.

As a result of malls' rapid growth, a whole support system and communication network has evolved. It includes the International Council of Shopping Centers — a mall business trade organization. Trade journals (scriptures?) such as *National Mall Monitor* and *Shopping Center World* are monthly magazines which feature articles on finance and investment, the science of shopping center management, innovations in merchandising, not to mention a plethora of advertisements for available leasing opportunities in malls nationwide. You will also find ads for special tile flooring, acoustical wood paneling, computer systems, and heating and air-conditioning services. In the mall trade journals you can even find advertisements for the finest in interior trees to provide "visual enhancement, functional placement, scale and proportion."

The malling of America illustrates further how much our economy depends on various services. Fast food restaurants provide employment for a large number of teenagers. Working at McDonalds or Burger King is now virtually a rite of passage for many high school students. Adults with an entrepreneurial spirit are attracted to leasing or owning franchises of various national chains. The burgeoning mall industry suggests that America is becoming a nation of shopkeepers.

• 3 •

The Shopping Mall
as Sacred Space

I believe one of the reasons malls have grown rapidly and their popularity increased is that they fulfill our need for order and orientation. Malling means centering. Yin-Fu Tuan, professor of geography at the University of Minnesota, says that "to be livable, nature and society must show order and display a harmonious relationship."[1] Or as philosopher of religion Paul Tillich said, we seek to "unify multiplicity."

The Nature of the Center

A theoretical framework from religious studies helps explain people's fondness for centeredness.* Human beings have always tried to center their lives and their world. Returning to the center has been a universal tendency, whether that center be a family reunion, a hometown, a native land, or a religious center such as Rome or Jerusalem.

This human propensity to design centers is illustrated by the prevalence of both circular construction and construction using such related shapes as hexagons, octagons, squares, and crosses. These geometric expressions reflect that same reality

*It will be obvious to many readers that the following discussion is dependent on the seminal works of Mircea Eliade and Paul Wheatley. Their contributions to the history of religions and human geography, respectively, are indispensable.

and have the same purpose: to incorporate all the dimensions of the earth — north, south, east, and west — the four corners of the world and the cardinal points of the compass.

The number four, incidentally, was a sacred number for many Native Americans precisely because of its all-embracing nature. The Native American shaman, Black Elk, observed that much of Indian activity — from drawing to dancing, to building their homes, whether tepee, hogan, or igloo — was done in a circle. The social and religious meeting place for the Navaho, a structure which connects this world with its place of origin, is the round ceremonial center called *kiva*.

This circular and cyclical activity was a reflection of the "power of the world" which worked in circles also; for example, the wind whirls, the seasons cycle, birds often fly concentrically, the sun and moon (both round) go and come in a circle. Everything tries to be round. The circularity of space for the Native American is also symbolized in the sacred hoop and the desire of every tribal member is to keep the hoop unbroken.

The inclusiveness of circular design echoes how we experience the world and perceive reality. These circles, squares, and crosses are a way of saying that the universe and, finally, our lives are symmetrical, well regulated, ordered, and under control.

The quadrilateral symbol, in whatever form, is a miniaturization of the world, a microcosm, a small picture of how we understand the larger universe to be. By this propensity to center, we are telling ourselves life is integrated and whole.

Centers are not only measured spatially and mathematically, they can be existential as well. The Quakers begin their silent meditation with the phrase "centering down" — that is, becoming stable, anchored, "together," to more easily get in touch with the cosmic center, the sources of stability and peace.

Communities have always centered themselves. Sometimes they have a functional center, as in many towns and villages laid out in the nineteenth-century, where there is a literal meeting of the quadrants at the town center. For example, you cannot avoid them if you drive through Harvard Square in Cambridge, Massachusetts or Gettysburg, Pennsylvania.

Other communities have ritual or ceremonial centers, such as parks, groves, or recreational areas. In religious studies we call such an area an axis mundi, the axle or pole around which our world turns and without which our world would collapse. These areas are indispensable to our personal and communal life. These centers are either built as a result of a hierophany (manifestation of the holy) or by ritual construction. Shopping malls are examples of the latter — what Mircea Eliade, the renowned religious historian at the University of Chicago, calls "mythic geometry."

The geometric designs in the mall also tell a story about how we ultimately understand the world to be; they are a replication of the larger planet. We have said by this paradigmatic structure that our experience of the world is one of balance and harmony. We have traveled to the "center" and discovered unity.

Carl Jung, the famous Swiss psychologist, calls the circle an archetype, an original image found in the collective unconscious of humankind. The pictures precede obviously the formulation and foundation of the living religions, but have appropriated these designs for their symbolic art and much of the architecture of their house of worship; for example, Buddhist stupas, Islamic mosques, Christian cathedrals, and Jewish temples and synagogues. Secular versions would be the Athenian agora, the Roman forum, the Mexican zocala, and the Middle Eastern bazaar.

The nature of the center gives us a clue to why so much human activity, from children's games to religious art and architecture to shopping malls, is expressed by circularity.

By applying the typology of Wheatley's and Eliade's "mythic geometry" to malls, we find a remarkable conformity and similarity between the design of the average mall and their models of sacred space.

Center as Source of Power

The number of people who gravitate to them indicate that centers are places of empowerment. Travelers, pilgrims, tourists, and shoppers departing from a center, find themselves renewed and strengthened as a result of the energy found there. Even if physically exhausted, their spirits are uplifted.

The axis mundi — whether it be a state capital, a religious shrine, or a mall as the social and shopping center of a community — becomes, to paraphrase Wheatley, "the pivot of ontological transition at which divine power enters the world and diffuses through wider territory."[2]

In this reduced version of the world, in this cosmos on a small scale where all life — human and natural — meet, you experience power coming from six directions: the four cardinal points of the compass and the zenith and nadir. To use Wheatley's graphic phrase, it is "an architectural evocation of an axis mundi."

Wheatley suggests that it is through such a center of the world that cosmic power enters and is spread throughout the country. This diffusion of energy binds "periphery and center, province and capital, dependencies and metropolitan territory."[3] This dissemination of power also established a unity of time and space. A community sense was created and maintained.

Paul Wheatley has abundant evidence in his *Pivot of the Four Quarters* that one reason gateways to traditional communities were large and ostentatious, out of all proportion to their function, was that power flowed out of the center through these entrances at the cardinal points.

Mall entrances, reflecting other significant centers of power, are often quite impressive. Their distinctiveness serves more than aesthetic, decorative, or functional purposes.

It is also interesting to watch the mall's capacity to balance centripetal and centrifugal forces. People are obviously drawn to this center and, just as effectively, the center delivers them back to the world with newly acquired treasures and relationships, if not a new sense of well-being.

When we are at the center, we can get our bearing, orient ourselves again, and find our way out of life's disorders. We discover at the center a source of power; this mirror of the universe concentrates the generally available dynamism.

Even in the midst of crowds, people are aware that a degree of renewal is taking place. Malls, at their centers, strive to be places of vitality and energy.

Consequently, it is not accidental that most places we call centers attempt to re-invigorate or recharge human energy. At both the personal and social levels, we find communities making such sources of power available.

This idea is ingrained in our language: New Windsor Conference Center, Baltimore Civic Center, Washington Heights Medical Center, Carroll County Agricultural Center, Aberdeen Shopping Center, Adams County Senior Center, Harford Recreational Center, Hagerstown Counseling Center, any number of college student centers, and religious worship centers. And so it goes. We find the concept of "center" an appropriate description for a place of human empowerment, a group of people who deliver social services, and an organization whose purpose is to help, heal, or otherwise improve the world.

This is undoubtedly what mall developer James Rouse has in mind when he uses the concept of center. His speeches and essays are replete with references to "center." He refers to the "design of the center," the "quality of the center," "little details of the center," and to "our center." Whatever else Rouse intends to convey, it is the human aspect of the center he wants to emphasize.

The center was originally understood to be where God and people and heaven and earth were connected. And power was generated there. We all know examples of these centers: the sacred mountains of Sinai and Zion, the cities of Benares and Mecca, the temples of St. Peter's in Rome and the Mormons in Salt Lake City, Utah. Church altars, dining room tables, and scholars' desks can also be centers of the sacred.

Such centers act as magnets. Their attractiveness is in direct proportion to the power and meaning we find there. We make regular pilgrimages to these special places to regain our identity, and to be reconnected, which, as I mentioned earlier, is the meaning of *re-ligare* (religion).

Center as Celestial Echo

Primitive people from Polynesia to Egypt to the British Isles were very careful in the construction of their centers. They found it extremely important to have, as a base for their center, a celestial or transcendent reference point and pattern. Eliade stresses there was usually some celestial archetype which provided a model for our earthly building and temporal construction, which would act as an axis mundi. And this other-worldly or heavenly counterpart would represent the true and authentic world. The heavenly Jerusalem, the historical Jerusalem, and the coming Jerusalem are all reflections of a city already found in the mind of God.

Eliade summarizes the inclination we have to reflect transcendent patterns in the construction of centers:

> "Man constructs according to an archetype. Not only do his city and his temple have celestial models, the same is true of the entire region that he inhabits, with the rivers that water it, the fields that give him his food, etc. The map of Babylon shows the city at the center of a vast circular territory bordered by a river, precisely as the Sumerian en-

visaged Paradise. This participation by urban culture in an arche-
typal model is what gives them their reality and validity."[4]

In one form or another, heavenly models are reflected in
earthly circularity.

Even the political centers of Paris, Washington, D.C., and
the centers (circuses) of London are further examples. It is
true, as well, of Dante's celestial rose, the thousand-petaled
Lotus of Buddhism, and the Tibetan Mandala.

The design and layout of most modern shopping malls is a
"secular" version of this ancient prototype. Many malls are
built in the form of a cross, with all paths leading to the center. The cross here is, of course, not the Christian cross or a
sectarian image. It is fundamentally a human image, for it is
another way of drawing a circle.

Knowing the frequency of circular patterns is more important than whether we know the engineer or architect's conscious and unconscious motivations for them. Circles in public buildings are symbols of welcome and inclusiveness, a way
to make our non-private space more humanly accessible. The
function of cardinal axiology, says Wheatley, is to assimilate
and bring together all the surrounding territory — which is to
say that the entire world meets in the center of every mall.

This sacred geometry can be seen in a representative sample of mall floor plans, gathered from across the country. And
even in the malls which do not have a symmetrical design, a
balance and harmony can be discerned in spite of the off-
centeredness. White Flint Mall in Rockville, Maryland is an
example of this.

If there is not a pronounced interaction at the center of the
mall as in Lancaster, Pennsylvania's Park City and Long Island's Smith Haven Mall, there may be a long corridor between rows of shops. In the center of the corridor may be
a series of pools or flower gardens surrounded by trees and
benches. Tampa Bay Center in Florida is a good illustration

SMITH HAVEN, *Long Island*
Here is a more simplified version of the square and cross forming a center. A floor plan and directory of shops are available for customers.

Name	Location
A. S. Beck Shoes	C18
Abraham & Straus	
Adler Shoes	C10
Amusement — Time Out	A30
Andre's	A25
Art Complete	A27
Asian Gift Shop	B8
Athletes Foot	B2a
Baker Shoes	B13
Barricini's	C11
Baskin Robbins	K-4
Beefsteak Charlie's	D6
Bell Yarn	A5
Brooks Fashion	D4
Buckner's	A3
Buster Brown	B7
Cardinal Ties	D11
Carol Jewelers	B12
Casual Corner	C15
Century Theatre	C1
Chandler Shoes	A7
Chess King	A10
Children's Outlet	D3b
Children's Photographer	K-8
Childrens Place	D3a
Churchill Music	A18
Cookie Factory	D6a
Craft Showcase	A1b
Cutlery Corner	K-7
Dalton Books	B2b
Different Stokes	C3
European-American Bank	A28
Express Pizza	B9
Fabrics Plus	C27
Family Melody Centers	C21
Fanny Farmer	C2
Father & Son Shoes	B11
Feet Street	C14
Feist & Feist Mgt. Agents	C108
Flagg Brothers Shoes	C12
Florsheim Shoes	D8
Fluf 'n' Stuf	K-6
Food of All Nations	A16
Foxmoor	A17
Frankel's	B15
Friendly Frost	A18
Friendly Ice Cream	B1
Fun Card & Gift	D15
G&G Shops	B19a
Gem Boutique Jewelers	D16
General Nutrition Center	B16
Hanover Shoes	A13

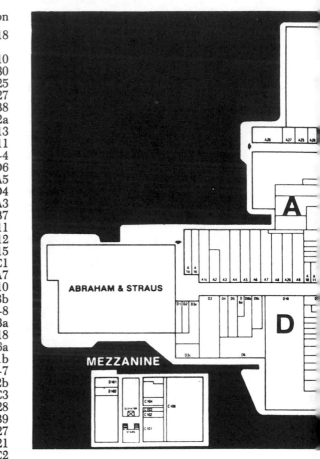

Name	Location
Hardy Shoes	D9a
Harwyn Family Shoes	A4
Herman's Sporting Goods	A22
Hillman Kohan Vision	A1a
Hodor Dinettes	C26
Holiday Health Spa	C5
Import Alley	B17
International Properties	C102
Intrigue Gifts	B5
Jewel Chest	K-2
Just Shirts	B10
Kay-Bee Toy & Hobby Shop	A31
Kid's Closet	A15
Kinney Shoe	C20

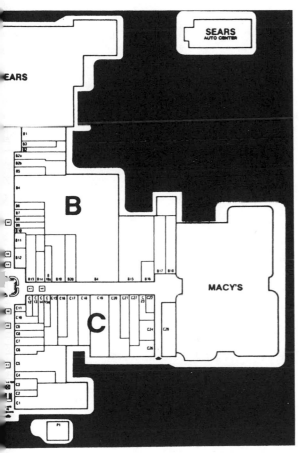

Name	Location
Merchants Association	C108
Michael's Trading Post	D20
Miles Shoes	C16
National Shirt Shop	C6
Naturalizer Shoes	C23
North Shore Numismatics	C103
Nuts 'n' Stuff	C13
Orange Julius	A11
Orlikoff (Dentist)	C104
Pants Place Plus	B18
Parklane	A23
Parklane	C22
Pretzel Stand	K-1
Regal Shoes	A12
Rite Aid Prescription Center	B20
Roaman's	A21
Rock Garden	B3
Rubin's Luggage	D14
Sam Goody	C17
Sbarro's	D18
Seamen's Bank for Savings	C29
Seamen's Bank for Savings	P1
Sears	
Sears Auto Center	
Sid's Slacks	A14
Sir Formal	C8
Smith Haven Card Shop	A6
Smith Haven Ministries	D101
Smith Haven Music	D1
Smith Haven Pet Center	B6
Spencer Gifts	D6c
Sterling Optical	D9
Stride Rite Nichols	C9
Strollers	K-3
Susie's Casuals	C7
Sylann's	B14
Tall Girl Shops-Shelly's	D12
Tempo Services	D102
The Gap	B19
Things Remembered	K-5
Thom McAn	A9
Time Out Amusement	A30
Tobacconist	C6
Ups and Downs	A8
Walden Books	D6b
Wallachs	D3
Walsh Conley	D2
Wicks and Sticks	A29
Wig Allure	A24
Wiss & Lambert	A20
Your Travel Agency	C15a
Zum Zum	C24

Name	Location
Lady Madonna	D10
Lafayette Radio	C4
Laidlaw-Coggeshall	A26
Lerner Shops	C19
Life Uniform	D13
Littman Jewelers	A2
Loeb Rhoades	C101
London Squire	A1c
Macy's	
Male Den	D17
Management Office	C108
Mankind	A16a
Martin's	D19
McCrory's	B4

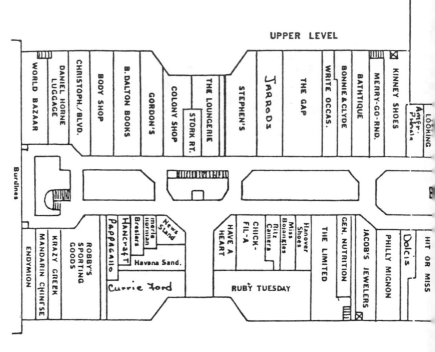

Tampa Bay Center
Although an elongated rectangle, this design shows again our propensity to center.

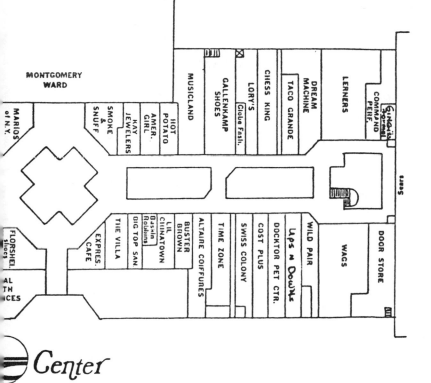

Center

ROSE WINDOW

Painton Cowen says that "every rose window is a symbol and image of the Creation and the created universe." Chartres' famous rose window is a triumph of geometry — an idealized model of the universe — circles within circles. Periphery and center are clearly depicted here. Dante's celestial rose and Buddha's thousand-petaled lotus are variations of this pattern. (Painton Cowen, *Rose Windows* (San Francisco: Chronicle Books, 1979). Photographic reproduction by Robert Boner.

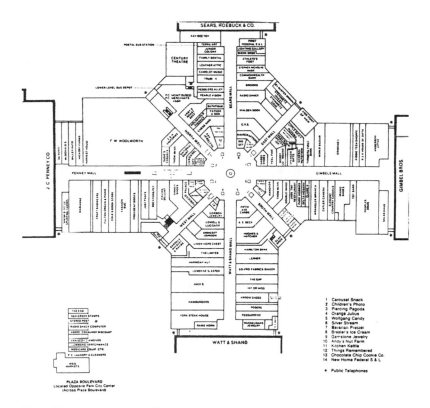

PARK CITY, *Lancaster, PA*
This mall reflects the many circles of a rose window, the quadrilateral design of a mandala, and the floor plan of typical cathedral or basilica. The center in this mall is inescapable.

NORTH STAR MALL, *San Antonio*
A time capsule is placed in the mall. Mall officials, visiting dignitaries, clergy, bands, and onlookers participate in this ritually significant occasion. This illustrates how space is sacralized. Courtesy, Rouse Co.

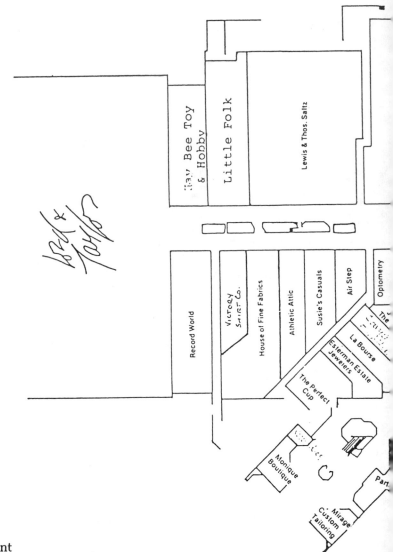

White Flint

WHITE FLINT MALL, *Rockville, MD*
We see here a certain balance, even if the floor plan is asymmetrical. It is obvious that the architect wants us to focus on the center.

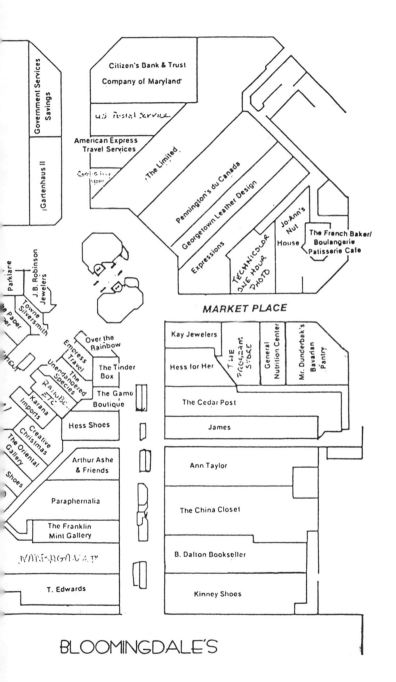

Government Services Savings

Gartenhaus II

Citizen's Bank & Trust Company of Maryland

U.S. Postal Service

American Express Travel Services

The Limited

Pennington's du Canada

Georgetown Leather Design

Expressions

TECHNICOLOR ONE HOUR PHOTO

Jo-Ann's Nut House

The French Baker/ Boulangerie Patisserie Cafe

Parklane

J.B. Robinson Jewelers

Towne Silversmith

Paper

MARKET PLACE

Over the Rainbow

Empress Travel

The Endangered Species

RARE ETC.

Karana Imports

Creative Christmas

The Oriental Gallery

Shoes

The Tinder Box

The Game Boutique

Hess Shoes

Arthur Ashe & Friends

Paraphernalia

The Franklin Mint Gallery

T. Edwards

Kay Jewelers

Hess for Her

The Cedar Post

James

Ann Taylor

The China Closet

B. Dalton Bookseller

Kinney Shoes

THE PROGRAM STORE

General Nutrition Center

Mr. Dunderbak's Bavarian Pantry

BLOOMINGDALE'S

of this pattern. Or, in the absence of a large visible center, smaller centers (crosses or circles) may be placed intermittently along the walkway.

Center as Sign of Order

As humans we have a profound need to repudiate, if not escape, the disorder and brokenness of life, and to establish islands of stability as a counterpoint to chaos. The creation of a center is usually the way people resist disorder. We always seem to be in the process of ordering (cosmicizing) — that is, making a whole (cosmos) out of disintegration (chaos). Indeed, the words for world in Latin (*cosmos*) and in German (*Welt*) suggest that in this place life is ordered by meaning and purpose. It is a uni-verse.

Practical activities, even the routine operation of a shopping mall, take second place to our need to see ourselves related appropriately to our environment. The so-called practical activities may offend the gods or spirits of nature unless they are perceived to have their roles in a coherent world system.[5]

We could not live long in an asymmetrical, chaotic community. Jung wrote an excellent monograph entitled *The Mandala. Mandala* is the Sanskrit word for a circle, divided into four separate, equal sections. It is really a symbol of the universe and Jung said that it is also a picture of the self. He discovered, in his clinical practice, that people of all ages who were emotionally disturbed or who were undergoing a certain degree of trauma, would often draw circular designs, presumably to reassure themselves that life is not radically ruptured. The innocent activity of our doodling often takes the shape of circles. At every level of human experience, the center must hold.

The re-creation of a center establishes order amidst chaos, serenity in turbulence, unity out of disparity, wholeness out of brokenness. The center, with all the paths leading to the middle, is a replication of the primordial world in all its harmony and pristine order.

Out of the disorder of the city and the dis-ease of the suburbs arises the shopping mall and its perceived symmetry and tranquility. People come to this center feeling isolated, lonely, and anonymous. They need to be at ease, to belong, to center themselves again. Chaos will be cosmicized. Disorder will be ordered.

Again, the mathematical balance, so frequently found in malls, is a way of reinforcing that the world is ultimately safe. The enclosure, combined with architectural balance, engenders the sense of safety many people claim they find in the mall.

Wheatley, in his extraordinary study on urban communities — construction from Mexico to Burma — has shown how order integrates space at several significant levels, e.g., global (cosmic), state (political), capital (ceremonial), and temple (ritual).[6] I want to add to this list of levels the shopping mall, a combination of the ceremonial and the ritual. As a result of their centered nature, their capacity to reveal and to communicate stability, malls juxtapose themselves to the mundane world outside. The outside world's profane dimension, according to Eliade, has no mythical meaning, is not invested with prestige, and lacks an exemplary model.[7] Or as John E. Smith, head of the philosophy department of Yale University, says, "The profane stands over against the holy, not because it is sordid or 'unclean,' but because it is ordinary and harbors no mystery, nor calls forth the sense that beyond and beneath our life is a holy ground."

To the extent that the mall is space discontinuous from the trivial, ordinary world, it is understood to be potentially sacred. The sacred is always more real than the profane and therefore more powerful than the ordinary world. As Eliade says in his *Sacred and Profane*, whatever is designated as sacred participates in and releases power. This power, in turn, puts us next to reality, which is tantamount to Being itself. This archaic ontology is reflected in the design of most malls and experienced by those for whom the mall is "more than" a collection of shops. There is a sense in which the mall is a space thought to be more real, vital, and energizing than the run-of-the-mill pragmatic world beyond it.

Perhaps this is why there is within us a "nostalgia for paradise" (Eliade), a longing for the village, a yearning for home or hometown, where life was more real and animated. This "more than" characteristic is perceived in malls and presents us with a sense of welcome, stability, and centeredness in which we can share vicariously.

Many shopping malls, as the foregoing reveals, are designed to repeat a cosmogony, that is, to re-create an ordered world. This is not to be taken lightly. As intellectual and social historian Eric Voegelin says, "The analogical repetition is not an act of futile imitation, for in repeating the cosmos man participates, in the measure allowed to his existential limitations, in the creation of cosmic order itself."[8]

So the mall attempts to make the world a whole, to have it integrated, habitable, safe, and balanced. Eliade, from a lifetime of studying the human fascination with the sacred, concludes: "To the degree that ancient holy places, temples or altars lose their religious efficacy, people discover and apply other geomantic architecture or iconographic formulas which, in the end, sometimes astonishingly enough represent the same symbolism of the "Center.""[9]

I contend that the mall represents, for many contemporary people, a substitute for those ancient sacred centers. If churches, schools, and families (our three major institutions) fail us, we will seek other places to fulfill basic human needs. It is not accidental, therefore, that malls contain the same structures, objects, and symbols which gave ancient centers their rich human meaning. For, as Eliade emphasizes, "images, symbols, and myths are not irresponsible creations of the psyche; they respond to a need and fulfill a function, that of bringing to light the most hidden modalities of being. Consequently, the study of them enables us to reach a better understanding of man — of man 'as he is.' " [10]

Symbols at the Center

Almost every shopping mall has a center court, the center of the center, the heart of the mall, its middle place and linchpin. This is the space which uniquely says that the mall is "more than" a marketplace. This meticulously planned and maintained space is, obviously, not essential for the exchange of goods and services. It is, in Wheatley's words, the "quintessentially sacred pivot." Specific symbols representing sacred geography are found at this juncture of spatial integration and natural harmony.

In some form, every mall has a center with the following: circles, squares, crosses, water, banners, art, sculpture, and vegetation (trees of various kinds, depending on the local climate, and potted plants, large and small).

Smith Haven Mall on Long Island and Francis Scott Key Mall in Frederick, Maryland are typical of malls which provide an area at or near the center for theater groups and instrumental or vocal musical groups. This space could be a slightly elevated stage or an amphitheater with two to four circular levels leading down to the performing area.

Some malls additionally display their own particular trademark in this central space. Countryside Mall in Clearwater, Florida has an ice rink; Prestonwood Town Center in Dallas has a magnificent thirty-three-foot-high grandfather clock; and Fox Hills in Los Angeles has an oriental garden with a glass and steel staircase which connects all levels of the mall.

The Prestonwood clock connects us with the past and illustrates how malls, while participating in the state of the art in

NORTH STAR, *San Antonio*
An excellent example of a center with fountain, stools, plants, trees, and flags. Courtesy, Rouse Co.

shopping and representing the efficiency of the computer era, want to link us to the "good old times." It was built in Boston in 1915 and brought to Prestonwood from Los Angeles in 1979. Public relations people there are anxious for you to read the brochure about the clock.

> We live in a modern age; we are accustomed to the feats of space travel, miracle medicines, heart transplants, computers that forecast the weather and beat us at a game of chess. We see TV news in color, of events that are happening at this instant, anywhere on earth. We see photographs of Jupiter and its many moons in revealing detail. But with all these incredible advances there are unfortunately some changes that diminish us. There is no longer a steam locomotive on the railroad, with its distinctive whistle and its display of might, or a fire engine with a brass bell, or a doctor who makes house calls. A lot of things from the good old time are disappearing fast. Luckily, there are some exceptions. . . . We feel that the Clock is a priceless inheritance and we do all we can to preserve it and give you the correct time. But more than that, the Clock adds something delicate and worthwhile to the atmosphere of the Prestonwood Town Center. It radiates a relaxing mood, a feeling of belonging to the past, present and future, all in one.

The clock is at the "center" of Prestonwood Town Center and they say that the easiest way to make a date at Prestonwood is to say, "Meet you at the clock."

This center of the center corresponds to a cathedral's sanctuary, the traditional space where the altar is found. The primary symbols of a religion are always found on or near the altar. Over the altar is an eternal flame or vigil light. You can usually find over a mall's center a huge skylight or a colorful and often circular series of lamps shedding such bright light over the center that you know you are in a space apart. That light, whether artificial or natural, accompanied by variously hued banners, is often so bright that it distinguishes the center from other areas of the mall.

This well-lighted center is a contemporary version of the

Roman atrium, the room in the center of a Roman house which was open to the sky. In fact, some mall designers call their mall just that—an atrium. The lighted center is also reminiscent of the courtyard in cloistered monasteries and the open public areas found in the colleges of Cambridge and Oxford universities and the commons of New England villages such as at Lexington, Massachusetts and New Milford, Connecticut. The porticoes, arcades, and walkways which surround them (and the centers of today's malls) mean that while people can walk either in or out of the sun, they always have direct access to light.

The landscaping along the corridors of the mall and around the center inevitably includes fountains, waterfalls, pools, rock gardens, trees, flowers, and plants. It is interesting to examine some of the details of this natural environment, especially water and trees.

Water of Life

Apart from using it to quench thirst, the main human experience of water is restoration, re-creation, and healing. ("He leads me beside still waters" and "He restores my soul," says David in Israel's ancient shepherd psalm.) This has been water's age-old attraction and appeal.

It is re-creative because our beginnings were in water. The Babylonian and Hebrew creation stories suggest that the world was created out of water; we are carried for nine months in amniotic fluid in the womb and when the "bag of waters" breaks, we are ready to be born; evolutionary theorists indicate that all of life emerged from the primordial ocean.

So, naturally, when people wanted to express the ultimate significance of water, they used such symbolic language as "Living Water," "Fountain of Youth," and "Water of Life" to describe it. It is said that this water flows from the "Throne of God," to indicate its divine origin. We consider water a gift, as well as knowing that it is indispensable for all life.

GRAND AVENUE, *Milwaukee*
The center of the center here reveals a stairway, statue, symmetrical design, and skylight. Courtesy, Rouse Co.

The traditional religious use of water has been primarily regenerative. Ritual bathing, baptism, lustration, and immersion in water are practiced by many religions. But the belief water has a life-giving and curative function is not limited to organized religion. Notice with what frequency we find in the eastern coastal states such places as White Sulphur Springs, Berkeley Springs, and Hot Springs. Another example is the purifying energy ascribed to the sand along the ocean shore at Virginia Beach, Virginia. These places for healing lustration are found throughout the country and, indeed, the world.

When water is united with vegetation, we are reminded of Eden, the prototypical garden, the enchanted glade—the place from which life sprang. There we lived with nature and knew the harmony of organic and inorganic reality. This yearning to re-establish our kinship with nature is reflected in the extremes to which communities go to make natural resources available for human enrichment. Large municipalities will provide parks and fountains in the midst of the busiest downtown areas to respond to the deeply felt need to live near and in relation to nature, even though we may be miles from a natural setting.

Mall developers have attempted ingeniously to satisfy this human longing to be near water. You can observe the various uses of water to be found in shopping centers. One mall, Strawberry Square in Harrisburg, Pennsylvania, has a small stream of water falling about fifteen feet into a pear-shaped metal pan tilted in such a way that water slowly runs out into a small pool. Another mall, Park City in Lancaster, Pennsylvania, has a fountain which, like Old Faithful in Yellowstone Park, gushes up eighteen or twenty feet into the air. The water falls into a pool with four outlets leading downward to a broader circular pool. The Galleria in White Plains, New York has a series of submerged pools with large rustic stones protruding from the surface, and at the center of Kenilworth

Bazaar in Baltimore there is a hexagonal pool which acts as a wishing well into which people throw coins.

Gwinnett Place outside Atlanta presents one of the country's most elaborate displays of water and foliage. This recently opened mall (February 1984) has a waterfall which descends about thirty feet over three levels of carefully masoned grey stone. The number of trees and the amount of water here remind one of a tropical forest.

The sound of falling or running water mercifully drowns out the din of the crowds and the pervasive sound of canned music. The fountain's sound gives you the sense of being outdoors and near the healing energy of natural forces.

In addition to fountains and waterfalls, some malls contain pools of water running along the walkways. There are often rocks in the pools, which are tree-lined. Bridges may enable the visitor to cross over the pool to another row of shops. Combine this with streetlights or chandeliers designed for electricity (sometimes with a gaslight effect), and you feel like you're in a colonial village. It is in such areas that people often stop to rest, meditate, or be still. In many instances it is peaceful, pastoral, relaxing.

Cosmic Tree

Shopping malls are amply supplied with the regenerative force of vegetation — foliage, green plants, trees, and flowers. And in a throw-away culture, where plastic often reigns, these plants are rarely artificial.

The tree is the classic symbol of vegetative life. As you undoubtedly know, there are two kinds of trees — the evergreen (signifying undying life) and deciduous which annually "die" and are "reborn." The budding of trees in the spring represents the re-constitution of all life. Both types of trees are signs of life in the presence of death. The Christmas tree, an evergreen, lives in the dark, death-filled winter as a sign that life will bloom again and days will lengthen in a few months.

BEECHWOOD, *Cleveland*
People gather around the center to eat, chat, read, and meditate. Courtesy, Rouse Co.

Arbor Day, usually celebrated in early May, is a time when trees are ritually planted. This activity may be an educational device to encourage youth to appreciate one of our valuable, renewable natural resources. But trees are also planted to commemorate a special event, to protest war and violence, and to gratefully acknowledge the return of a loved one. Water and trees stand for life.

Our health of mind and body is restored by close proximity to our natural relatives, or as St. Francis of Assisi would say, our mother, father, brother, and sister. In this proximity we verify what the twentieth century Asian Indian poet, Rabindranath Tagore, affirmed: "The same stream of life that runs through my veins night and day runs through the world and dances in rhythmic measures."

Of course, there are no seasons in the mall. So even if there are not evergreen trees such as fir, spruce, or pine, the trees found there are bred to be green all year. Inside the enclosed air-conditioned mall, summer and winter are indistinguishable. You only know the seasons by way of the exhibits, store windows, and other displays which might reveal appropriate sale items for that particular season.

Lenox Square in Atlanta has an orchard of seventy crab apple trees in rows which serve as dividers in the parking lot. The garden effect begins as soon as you park your car. The trees collectively recall the Cosmic Tree or Tree of Life — the vitality and continuation of life or, as Eliade puts it, "the world as living totality."

It is startling to consider both the imagination and capital which mall designers and developers have invested in reproducing natural settings. These efforts tell of something in us not prefaced by a dollar sign.

Interestingly, malls often incorporate a reference to nature, e.g., dale, lake, wood, brook, marsh, and park. Some characteristic names are:

Brookhaven   Southdale
Northpark   East Lake
White Marsh   Prestonwood

Often these malls may not be near any of the natural environments suggested by their names. It might be concluded
that the natural reference in the name points instead to an
ambience you can expect inside the mall. The possibility of
being re-united with nature, while ostensibly shopping, still
continues to attract us.

Frequently the center of a mall resembles a park or shaded
grove, with walkways, bandstands, gazebos, benches and
tables where picnics can be held year round. (One expects a
hawker to come along any moment and announce the sale of
peanuts, popcorn, hot dogs, cotton candy, and soda pop.)

The more cynical might suggest that the center simply per-
forms a practical function. It cuts down the amount of walking needed. People from the edge of the parking lot will be
equidistant from the mall if it is in the center of the lot and,
once inside, equidistant from the center court if the mall's
four cardinal points meet in some symmetrical pattern.

But there is really a more profound and symbolic message
in all of this. The importance to the human mind of a center
was established prior to language. It is in our nervous system as a race or, as Jung writes, our collective unconscious.
And the collective unconscious is the source of these original
images.

From a history of religions perspective there are good reasons for both the presence of the center and all those symbols
found there. They are a response to our fundamental need to
remember our affinity with nature and to return periodically
to a stable world. The contemporary mall documents the pervasive and practical expression of this response.

Human Activity at the Center

While behavior varies at the mall's center, there are certainly definite patterns of human interaction. One of the most interesting exercises is to view — with some empathic scrutiny — the social behavior of people at the center court.

The center, first of all, provides a place to rest. People sit on chairs, benches, or steps to relax their bodies and minds from extended walking and standing. The tensions and pressures of shopping — trying to discover a bargain, being frustrated at not finding the proper size or label for a child — afford sufficient reason for "time out" at the center.

Other visitors to the center court want to escape the hectic pace experienced at other times of the day, in or out of the mall. I have talked with clerks, waiters, and waitresses who find some temporary relief by taking their break at the center. Two young female clerks who work in a gift shop said, "Here's where we take a 'psych-break' from grumpy customers." If you are confined to the mall, or have no other such center, there is a desire to seek out a place where a certain healing can occur. The psycho-physical props of the center, including its geometrical design, water, and trees, help harried customers regain a sense of balance.

Other things may be done while resting. A number of people read books and newspapers; some play cards or checkers with friends; others engage in conversation, often in small groups; still others wait for friends or relatives who have not finished shopping.

Many people gather at the center to stare, almost zombie-like. At times these stares are interrupted by the sight of a crying child tended by his or her grandmother or a strolling group of teenagers. Then they find themselves again watching people and focusing on the passing parade.

Yet the blank faces and unfocused gazes often reveal the loneliness and isolation of some mall visitors. Upon entrance they're drawn instinctively to the center in hope of diversion. This gravitation toward the center implies an expectation that, as a result of being there, thoughts will be collected and perhaps lives will be a bit more anchored. This form of activity verges on meditation. It is clear that a small portion of congregants at the center are intentionally engaging in this type of religious exercise. I recall a woman who had been sitting at the edge of a center for about forty minutes. She was hidden from most of the public by a large potted plant. She said, "This is my time of recollection." I mentioned to her, "That is a word used by religious people when they speak of re-gaining wholeness." She replied, "That is exactly what I am doing."

Children playing generates another form of activity altogether. The area's openness and what certainly appears to them to be a vastness of space, impels them to run, jump, tumble, and shout. Many malls predicted that children would gather at the center, either with their parents or in groups. They consequently planned small playgrounds with jungle gyms and other assorted objects for crawling on and through. This area, in many malls, seems as natural a part of the center as the concert stage, fountains and trees.

Another form of human interaction at the center involves couples, of all ages, who sit and talk together. Self-conscious teenagers huddle in small groups around the center to compare the latest fads and, away from the sanctions of parents and teachers, to share frankly their thoughts and feelings about issues of life-and-death importance to them. In contrast to the highly energized conversations of the youth, older couples, in a more leisurely way, exchange stories and small talk.

Community at the Center

The phrase "meet you at the mall" has become part of our language. Although community is, by definition and experience, not something we create, the mall has been successful in fostering a sense of community. Regardless of the negative judgments made against them, malls are indisputably an alternative to the ennui and isolation found in urban and suburban America.

That so much time beyond home and work is spent in the mall underscores that we are looking for social relations. This investment of our energy and time is a statement about our need for community. In a society where there are so many meetings where people do not meet and personal relationships in which nothing personal takes place, the mall, for good or ill, has filled a vacuum.

Studies by mall developers show that up to 40% of people coming to malls do not intend to buy anything. They come to browse, window shop, and pass the time. Most of these people may, incidentally, buy something or purchase a snack or meal, but their purpose was to experience the "more than" of that marketplace. In fact, about 90% of people entering malls end up spending some money there.

What Jim Pettigrew, Jr., writing in *Sky* magazine, said of the current attempt to renovate waterfronts in urban areas can appropriately be said of malls. "They can easily become magnets of humanity, with these 'people places' providing valuable relief from the hectic automated pressure of contemporary urban life."[11]

Centers, in some form or another, natural or fabricated, imply community, just as community was implicit in the village square, the New England common, and Saturday night in Bel Air. Malls, as human centers, try to convey that they are places where people want to be, can feel at home, and to which they will want to return.

There is little doubt the mall has provided an alternative community for many and perhaps is the only community for some. Two anecdotes recounted by James Rouse illustrate well this fulfillment of communal need.

A banker friend in Boston said to me the other day, "Faneuil Hall Marketplace has introduced a whole new element into our family life. We now come downtown on a Saturday afternoon to the market, have dinner, spend the evening. My children are beginning to learn about the city and care about it." And a cab driver the other morning in Boston, in reply to my question, "What do you think of Faneuil Hall Marketplace?" replied: "It's the best thing that has ever happened to the city of Boston." "Why do you say that?" I asked. "Because it's done more for the people of the city than anything that's happened. I'm an old man," he said. "My wife died two years ago. I haven't had much to do. Now on Sunday after church, I go down to the market, spend the afternoon, have supper. I look forward to it all week."[12]

In my travels, a woman in Georgia said, "The mall is a good meeting place for lunch. I come here at least twice a week." A retired businessman, living in Florida, said, "My wife and I come here three times a week. I sit on the bench, watch people, and read a lot. It's weather-protected and always clean."

In their brochures, ads, and billboards, mall promoters hold out the lure of a special "experience" you will have in their shopping area. Their human appeal is finally the "more than" of elegance, excitement, and graceful luxury combined with a "down home" folksiness. Malls seek to woo the public in the name of community with such quotes as:

"you are part of us."

". . . devoted to eating, shopping and the pursuit of happiness."

"You are going to love the experience."

"It's yours to enjoy."

"Explore and savor the delightful potpourri of over 200 fine shops, restaurants, and services."

"We want to make a good impression (and the 'O' in impression is a large fingerprint), so we touch your life individually, uniquely, and personally with our very own fingerprint. We can identify with all your needs and provide a pleasurable shopping atmosphere."

"Where good things happen . . ."

Let's allow for the seduction, the hyperbole, the "come on," and the overblown and impossible-to-keep promises. But behind these words are messages and notions of providence, well-being and a possible human community. Unsaid in these public relations statements is the reality that people may go to malls to buy there, but they also go to "be there."

Community Services for the Whole Person

In most malls, a variety of services are offered which goes well beyond shopping in the usual sense. The availability of these services expands the notions of "one-stop shopping" so popular with mall marketing specialists. Health services are provided, and dental offices and medical clinics are often present. Ancillary health care can also be found in the form of saunas, spas, and the health clubs, as well as in aerobics classes sponsored by the local YWCA and YMCA. Aerobics classes, along with courses in karate and in Tai Chi, are often conducted along the walkways or near the center court and give the benchsitting people-watchers an extra treat. Coin-operated biorhythm and blood pressure machines are usually available also. Malls are providing the opportunity for an increasing number of physicians to set up medical clinics. It is the contemporary version of the house call.

Business services—like auto agencies, real estate offices and life insurance agents—are available. Electronic bank teller machines, as well as traditional banking facilities, also can be found.

Sensitivity to the needs of consumers prompts mall managers to provide child care through renting strollers. Sometimes, babysitting services and a playroom for children are also available. A daycare center is provided by Crossroads Mall in Boulder, Colorado. Loaning of wheelchairs to the disabled and the elderly is another important service offered.

Spiritual and emotional counseling is a final set of human services found in the mall. It is not unheard of to find chapels where you can meditate and even get married. William Kowinski found John XXIII Chapel in Monroeville Mall in western Pennsylvania where mass is celebrated daily. A ministry of counseling and listening is also associated with these services. The clergy involved in this ministry are invariably flexible, liberal, and people-oriented. These ministers and priests are enablers and affirmers who help people "turn the corner" of whatever minor crisis they bring with them. Proselytizing would be inappropriate.

Many larger malls publish their own monthly newsletters and newspaper sales supplements to publicize more fully the wide range of personal and public services they offer. These services have proven beneficial, not only to the persons in need, but also to the mall. Customers profit from having their many levels of needs met and malls profit financially.

An earlier trend in malls, from their inception to about the middle 1970s, was to plan performances by sensational entertainers, including some top movie and television personalities. They were considered bait to lure customers. Now mall managers have exchanged excitement for wisdom and find that people are attracted by efforts to meet a wide spectrum of human needs — health, business, spiritual, and personal — and so the plethora of athletic clubs, counseling kiosks, consumer advocate offices. The idea is that the whole person is important and "one-stop shopping" can include more than purchasing commodities.

Community as Meeting of Persons

Centers have a way of transcending differences. The experience at the center is usually one of unity. Just as the spokes of a wheel are closer to each other as they get nearer to the hub, so people, as they get closer to the center, are closer to each other.

This community can be tested empirically. The people who congregate around the pools, fountains, and trees at the center are invariably approachable and responsive. The natural environment helps them to be receptive. In the presence of nature — and aided by the carefully calculated positioning of furniture — we do feel more accessible to each other.

In some cases, it is as if you were in a Parisian sidewalk cafe or, in rare instances, in someone's living room — so fluid is the space between walkway, seating, and shops. The mall is "in you and you are in it." There are no clear-cut lines drawn between shoppers, conversationalists, strollers, and diners. This special use of place is not threatening, but rather gives a patron the sense of ease and welcome. The atmosphere is often so relaxed that children know intuitively they have permission to play their unrehearsed, unorganized games.

All ages tend to come to the malls, but teenagers and the elderly are most in evidence. The average age of the intentional consumer is approximately 25–50. So the mall provides the strongest sense of community for teenagers and older persons.

I have noticed that elderly folks tend to visit the mall in the morning to avoid the under-18 crowd which converges there after school. In fact, these age groups form two discernible subgroups in the mall. These groups form the mall's closest approximation of a primary community. This significant human networking cannot be dismissed.

Both young and old are at the shopping center to escape their respective worlds of loneliness — the young from fear of being alone, excluded, and different, and the elderly from boredom and lack of companionship. I asked teenagers why they come to malls. The most frequent responses were "to hang out," to check out the guys, and to watch the girls. One young man said, "It's a cool place to come to escape the house." A young woman, who had clerked for three years in a shoe store in a northern Virginia mall, told me that young people (mostly girls) would come in and try on shoes by the hour — as an alternative to boredom.

Nowhere is the ceremonial interaction of the young more visible than in the mall. Hip-hugging, thigh-tight jeans are ritual garments for both sexes in this community as individuals wander into the world of sexual relationships. It is a place, away from home, where hands are held timidly, cigarettes first smoked or drugs first sampled. The sheer excitement of these furtive dalliances and the accompanying suspension of formal and traditional behavior patterns encourage this experimentation. This activity may progress to dating, which is also ritualized at the mall. After getting a drivers' license, the youths no longer frequent the mall to "hang out" — they have other places for that — but they may return to the mall for a movie.

Older folks have other needs. They are here for diversion, to walk and to talk with peers. Women in small groups will windowshop or browse, while men, often their husbands, will gather around tables or on circular benches near the fountain, to chat or play cards. I remember one small group of older men sitting together in Tyrone Square Mall in St. Petersburg, Florida. One of them said, with concurrence from the rest, "I am not interested in going in and out of shops. I never did it when I was young — no use starting now. I'm doing just fine waiting here for her." It's all reminiscent of the male bonding and socializing that took place around the cracker barrel and pot-bellied stove in the old country store or in the park in Bel Air. It is a reflection of the rigid gender role socialization of the generation of men and women now in retirement. They feel more comfortable interacting socially with members of the same sex. So we find that the mall is the only real place for a lot of Americans to meet other people.

On the other hand, a good many people don't socialize. The mall is not the small town in which they grew up amid the intimacy of a face-to-face, ongoing community. As you watch people sitting on benches, you'll notice that they sit carefully, facing away from the person with whom they are sharing the bench. At times they will stare, their faces blank and listless. They seem to desire their own private space and time. Near the vegetation and water, they enter into themselves and get in tune again with their internal rhythms.

Then again, there are some people who are remarkably open to relative strangers and when casually approached, will light up with gratitude for being recognized. And, when the same people come on a regular basis, something approaching a primary community emerges. This can become an integral part of those individuals' week.

Perhaps this sounds like I'm idealizing the sense of community found in the average mall. To be sure, the community mentioned is to a large extent fabricated, artificial, and contrived. It is not a natural, personal, organic community. But the mall, apparently, is so effective an approximation of the fulfillment of human social needs that it is a viable communal setting for many of our citizens. It may be the only working and workable expression of community for a sizable segment of our population.

High Touch of Shopping

In 1984 author Isaac Asimov said, "(Computers) can be used to place orders with your broker, travel agent, banker, or at the shopping mall."[13] There is doubt, however, that malls will disappear because, at least for now, they are more than places to shop. They are also places for us to experience social reality.

In fact, John Naisbitt, in his best-selling *Megatrends: Ten*

Directions Transforming Our Lives, reinforces this observation in a chapter entitled, "From Forced Technology to High Tech/High Touch." Naisbitt contends that "whenever new technology is introduced into society, there must be a counter balancing human response — that is, high touch — or the technology is rejected." The more high tech, the more high touch, he says.[14]

He goes on to say that the built-in contradiction to high tech is the need for people to be together. He cites the shopping mall as an example of that urge to congregate in the face of more and more technology and, in effect, asks if this is why shopping malls are the third most frequented place in our lives.

While acknowledging that we will soon shop by computer, Naisbitt limits this shopping to staple items identified clearly in advance. "It will be no substitute for the serene dignity and high touch of shopping for what we want to be surprised about." The shopping mall, being more than a marketplace, will remain intact. The Bell Telephone system, of course, has cleverly co-opted this balance of high tech/high touch with its "Reach out and touch someone" campaign.

Finally, this stress on human community and the need we have for solidarity with one another is a religious expression. We have said earlier that religion essentially implies a re-binding, re-connection, and re-union. Even though malls are ritually constructed centers and do not have their origins in the organic life of a natural human community, our attraction to them is an indication of the urge, and sometimes desperation, we have to belong to a wider group, to be known by others, and to retain our identity as members of the human family.

Community Outreach

When James Rouse asked a high school principal in Cherry Hill, New Jersey what the new Cherry Hill Center (mall) meant to the community, he said: "Personal standards of the students had been noticeably lifted by the standards of the Center." And a high school girl said that until Cherry Hill Center was built there was no sense of community in the area.

The more successful malls try to relate to the wider community rather than just concentrating on merchandising efforts. Some mall managers and marketing specialists ask, "What are the recreational, cultural, educational needs in the community that we can meet?" There is always the hope of attracting customers, but many malls want the community to feel enriched by their presence.

To this end, program directors, public affairs coordinators, and community relations officers are hired to assure that the mall is responsive to the peripheral community's needs. These marketing professionals will send out mass mailings two to four times a year inviting various social groups to hold fund drives, participate in promotions, and provide entertainment for certain seasonal celebrations. Christmas, of course, is the season most visibly celebrated and the time when the mall is most connected to the wider community.

Civic, cultural, and community events are promoted, as well as the mall's own commercial events. Some mall managers are quite sincere about their relations to the community and the community's involvement in the ongoing life of the mall. Still, it is perhaps a pale reflection of Stanley Preston in Bel Air, who put people first and saw business success as a by-product.

Strawberry Square in Harrisburg, Pennsylvania proves an interesting example of how one mall extends itself to the neighboring community. It is difficult to distinguish the events which are community "services" of the mall from those which the community provides to the mall for entertainment.

Strawberry Square's (1983) annual report lists its efforts to be of service to the community. Programs are divided into "large scale events" and "Fund raisers/Promotions." Such activities may last from one day to a week depending on their

---

THE PLACE WILL TICKLE EVERYONE'S FANCY WITH ENTERTAINMENT AND MERRIMENT THROUGHOUT THE MONTH OF FEBRUARY

CALENDAR OF EVENTS

Wednesday, February 1
Grand Opening Gala

9:00am — Doors open
9:15am — 530th Air Force Band, Ga. Air Nat'l Guard, Dobbins Air Force Base, Georgia
9:35am — Gwinnett Choral Guild
9:45am — Official Opening Ceremonies
10:00am — Ribbon Cutting, mall opens
10:00am-1:00pm — Balloons and feathers given away
10:00am-4:00pm — Great American Mime Experiment
7:00pm — Callenwolde Concert Band

Thursday, February 2
Down-home Sampler

1:30pm-4:30pm — Greater Atlanta Bluegrass Band
5:00pm — Calico Clickers Cloggers
6:30pm — Sweet & Sassy Cloggers (National Champions)
8:00pm — Dahlonega Mountain Band

Friday, February 3
A Touch of Europe

1:30pm-4:00pm — Great American Gypsy Band
5:00pm-8:00pm — Shirley Jobin, strolling accordionist
7:00pm — Izvorni Folk Ensemble
8:00pm — Atlanta Pipe Band

Saturday, February 4
Carnival Capers

12:00pm-8:00pm — Great American Mime Experiment
12:30pm-2:00pm — Margaret Lemon, juggler
1:00pm-3:00pm — WQXI Quaker
2:00pm-4:00pm — Chief Nockahoma, Atlanta Braves mascot. Falcon player and mascot, autographing session
3:00pm-5:00pm — Georgia Tech Yellow Jacket Mascot
3:00pm — Dan the Wizard, magician
3:00pm-5:00pm — Margaret Lemon, juggler
4:00pm-6:00pm — Rocky Raccoon
5:00pm-8:00pm — UGA "Hairy" Dog
6:00pm-8:00pm — Margaret Lemon, juggler
7:00pm — Dan the Wizard, magician

Sunday, February 5
Casual Classics

2:00pm-4:30pm — Thomas O'Donnell & Friends (Atlanta Symphony Players Association)

Thursday, February 9
South of the Border Fiesta

4:00pm-7:00pm — Fiesta Mariachis (strolling Mexican band)
7:30pm — Columbian Folkloric Dance Group of Atlanta

Friday, February 10
Dixieland Delights

1:00pm-4:00pm — Ruby Red's Dixieland Jazz Band
6:30pm-8:30pm — Capital City Jazz Band

Saturday, February 11
Salute to America

12:00pm — Fulton Community Band
2:00pm — Backstage Dancers salute American dance
3:00pm — Gadabouts Barbershop Quartet
4:00pm — Backstage Dancers (encore performance)
7:00pm — Atlanta Peachtree Barbershop Chorus

Sunday, February 12
Elegant Atlanta

1:00pm-3:00pm — Renaissance Atlanta players
3:30pm — Cabaret Alliance
4:30pm — Theatrical Outfit

Saturday, February 18
Caribbean Getaway

2:00pm — Drawing for an exotic cruise and a spa membership
3:00pm-5:00pm — The Celebrities, featuring The Tamboo Steel Band
6:00pm-8:00pm — The Tamboo Steel Band
7:00pm — Claude Fabian, and his Caribbean dancers

Sunday, February 19
Glorious Gwinnett

1:30pm — Georgia Baton & Dance Studio Twirlers (State Champions)
2:30pm — Possum Trot Cloggers
4:00pm — Gwinnett All County Theater Association Road Show "Salute to Gwinnett"

ALL PERFORMANCES last one hour or less unless otherwise noted.

A month-long schedule of events for the Grand Opening of Gwinnett Place in Atlanta. There are art forms, fun, and festivity to please a variety of tastes. It is easy to see how this mall tries to identify with the surrounding community.

popularity and the needs they serve. Most of the large-scale events receive a good deal of media coverage.

A sampling of large-scale events includes:

— Senator John Heinz — Town Meeting
— Harrisburg Area Road Runners — Registration and Awards Ceremony
— Dauphin County Area Agency on Aging and American Red Cross — Senior Fun Day
— A wedding reception
— A bridal shower
— Pennsylvania Historical and Museum Commission: 80 displays from state students on "Turning Points in History"
— Central Pennsylvania Spay/Neuter Fund: Poster Contest and Awards Ceremony
— Central Pennsylvania March of Dimes: Annual Balloon Launch
— River Rescue of Harrisburg, Inc.: Proclamation, speeches, and demonstrations
— Dauphin County Retarded Citizens Association
— Bar Mitzvah reception
— Pennsylvania Black Heritage Alliance: Jazz and Poetry by local artists
— Celebrity Dial-a-Thon for South Central Pennsylvania Heart Association
— Parents without Partners: Awards presentation
— Encyclopedia Britannica Story Telling

In addition, the following community groups held fund raisers in Strawberry Square during that year: West Shore Elks, Pennsylvania National Guard, Animal Haven, Arthritis Foundation, Harrisburg Exchange Club, Holy Name Church, Retired Senior Volunteer Program, Jewish Community Center, V.F.W. Post 31, Hemlock Girl Scout Council, and Zion Lutheran Church.

One of the very latest trends in community outreach is the

Girl Scout Sleep-In. Jumpers Mall near Washington, D.C. and Columbia Mall in Maryland have sponsored these all-night pajama parties.

Elizabeth Wallace, mother of one of the girl scouts, sent me her account of the event in March of 1985 at Columbia Mall.

Girls will arrive at the Mall at 10:15 PM; 38 troops have registered for the event (registration was held during 10 days in December). Each troop will be given a location on the upper level of the mall to stash sleeping bags and supplies. At 11 PM, an opening ceremony will be held for all 650 girls and 250 adults attending. And from 11:15 on, the girls will be able to choose from over 25 different activities: among them, weaving, quilting, square dancing, relays, needle-point, manicuring, origami, macrame, arts and crafts, aerobics, solar cooking, or face painting. During the night, song workshops and badge workshops will be held. Scouts can make terrariums or face masks.

While certain areas of the huge Columbia Mall will be off-limits (and over 50 security Dads will be on duty to keep it that way), within those limits the girls will have complete freedom of movement. Each girl will be required to have a buddy at all times, but in pairs of two, girls can attend any workshop or program activity they choose, in any order they choose. A rest period will be enforced between the hours of 4 and 6 AM during which time girls must stretch out quietly on their sleeping bags: they do not have to sleep and are encouraged to bring books or quiet games along to use during this time. Of course, girls can retire to their sleeping bags at any time during the night; theoretically, a scout could sleep from 11:15 PM until 7:15 AM if she chose to do so; adults will be posted throughout the upper sleeping level at all times and since all programs take place on the lower level, the sleeping area should be relatively quiet.

The Mall staff has been most helpful and cooperative in the planning of the event, donating sound equipment for opening and closing ceremonies, and guaranteeing that all entrances to the Mall will be sealed at 10 PM. Any theatres or restaurants still open at that time are sealing their exits into the Mall and requiring patrons to exit directly onto the parking lot. Several food vendors will be staying open for the event, however, so that the girls attending can purchase pizza, ice cream, and other such slumber party staples.

> At 7:15 AM a short closing ceremony will be held. Then each troop will clean up its own camp-out area, and once it has passed inspection, check out.

An increasing option provided by malls is college courses for academic and continuing education credit. Students "learn and shop" at the Castleton Shopping Mall in Indianapolis, Indiana.

Some malls permit voter registration drives to be conducted on the premises: radio and television stations will often air special programs from the mall; members of local professional athletic teams will appear at the mall to meet their fans, sign autographs and chat with customers. Indeed, women interested in becoming cheerleaders for the Baltimore Stars football team auditioned recently in Hunt Valley Mall near Baltimore.

Most of these events are held at or near the mall's center. Receptions and more private meetings are held in the mall's conference or community room. These facilities are almost essential in malls built in the last decade and are evidence that mall developers and managers see themselves as part of the larger community.

It is worth noting that as the mall phenomenon grows and malls are increasingly understood to be community centers, large communities are growing around them. In the last few years, malls have been planned and built as hubs of future commercial cities.

For example, Gwinnett Place outside of Atlanta expects, in the next ten years, to be surrounded by a complex of commercial and residential buildings, including condominiums, offices, hotels, conference centers, and a series of satellite malls. These multi-dimensional complexes are being called omnicenters. One of the first examples of this trend was Chicago's Water Tower Place, with its high-rise structures, hotels, and medical offices.

Gwinnett Place planners predict that it will be the center

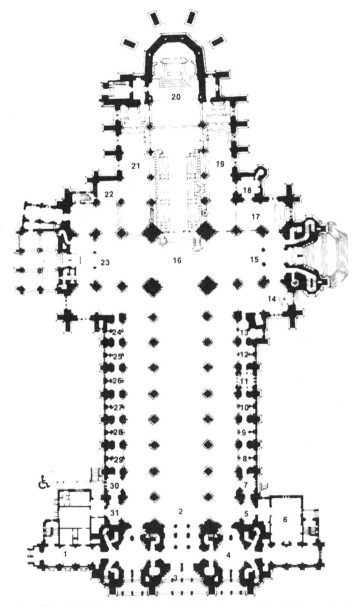

Floor plan of the Washington Cathedral, Washington, D.C. The cathedral proper illustrates symmetry created by the use of crosses and squares—a fine example of cardinal axiology found in many malls. As one enters the building eyes are drawn immediately to its center, the altar. Used by permission of Washington Cathedral.

of what will happen in the surrounding area. Community growth, in terms of these buildings, will follow the construction of a huge mall. A wider community will develop with a certain dependence on the mall. Power will come in and out of that center in centripetal and centrifugal ways. Gwinnett Place, and other such construction, remind us that many cities began as trading centers or religious shrines. And traditional societies rarely distinguished between these functions.

Twenty-five years ago, sociologist of religion Gibson Winter wrote about the "suburban captivity of the church." "White flight" and economic upward mobility glutted the perimeter of cities. People who moved to the suburbs were disoriented and without roots. Churches were built in the same unimaginative "ticky-tacky" style as the rows of houses. The hope was that the churches would provide orientation and a sense of community. They did so for relatively few suburbanites, and mostly on Sundays.

The shopping mall, open almost every day from 10 A.M. to 9 P.M., became the place of orientation and the community center for many others. Since churches appeal mainly to ideological, sectarian, and class interests, it became and remains largely an exclusive organization. The combination of festivity, ritual, and commerce make the mall as equally a significant, if not a more inclusive and egalitarian, center as most churches. This is, essentially, the vision of James Rouse.

Transition: James Rouse — Mahatma of Malls

In moving from a discussion of the shopping mall as sacred space to reflections on the mall as sacred time, I would like to review the life and thought of the one man whose name is synonymous with shopping malls.

James Wilson Rouse is the Mahatma (Great Soul) of malls and the guiding spirit of these commercial and cultural enterprises. Although he has preferred to focus the limelight on his projects — Columbia City (Howard County, Maryland), Cherry Hill Mall (New Jersey), Harborplace (Baltimore), Faneuil Hall (Boston), South Street Seaport (New York City), Waterside (Norfolk, Virginia) — there is no question that he is the genius, innovator, inspiration, and creative energy behind the growth of the enclosed shopping mall in the 1950s and 1960s and the revitalization of downtown areas by way of festival marketplaces in the 1970s and 1980s. He and his company have been responsible for about sixty malls and marketplaces.*

Let us begin with what this man considered to be the Rouse Company "creed" when he was head of the organization. It is found in a speech he gave in 1979 upon his retirement as chief executive officer of the company. The "creed" begins with the "conviction that what we do is of enormous importance." The

---

*Actually, the company has built about forty malls and acquired twenty from other sources. Nine malls are now on the drawing board including Riverwalk in New Orleans and Bayside in Miami.

James Rouse died on April 9, 1996.

statement of belief, here somewhat paraphrased, continues with the following convictions:

— that the lives of people and communities for generations to come will be affected by what we do;

— that the surest road to success is to discover the authentic needs and yearnings of people and do our best to service them;

— that people seek warm and human places with diversity and charm, full of festival and delight, and that they are degraded by tacky, tasteless places and are oppressed by coldness and indifference;

— that they are uplifted by beauty and order and made significant by the creative caring which that demands;

— that we believe everything matters, that all detail is important.

Rouse then adds that this way of thinking is the "surest way to long-term values, to growth in earnings, and to escalating reward for service rendered."[1] This affirmation of faith informs all that the company did as well as why and how they did it, under his leadership.

How could a modern businessman facing severe competition practice such a creed? The answer can be found in Rouse's more than three dozen printed speeches (he has, of course, made hundreds). Four distinct themes prevail.

The first is his willingness to dream, to think big, or, to use one of his favorite phrases, "to make no little plans." He is a visionary, but a practical visionary. He is an optimist, but a realistic optimist. He is a liberal, but a pragmatic liberal. He is a dreamer, but one who wants to see his dreams actualized in the most concrete way in the American city.

Rouse combines what theologian ethicist Kenneth Cauthen calls "technological reason and visionary reason." "Technological reason, by its sheer power, affects our individual destinies every day in many ways. On the other hand, visionary reason, with its goals and values, guides our entire life."[2]

Since Rouse understands that technological reason should be the servant of visionary reason, he produces a healthy balance which Cauthen says exists "between efficiency and ecstasy."

Second, James Rouse is a humanist; he believes in people and their capacities, in what they can produce if they put their minds to it. It was difficult for his colleagues to share his belief that people were first and profits second. But this conviction allowed Rouse to imagine the humanization of marketplaces in particular, as well as life in general, in large urban communities.

Also, this affirmation of people found natural expression in his commitment to racially integrated housing in his city of Columbia, Maryland. He even co-authored a small book in 1955 entitled *No Slums in Ten Years*. When he was building Columbia in the mid-1960s, he forecast that blacks would not be subject to discrimination in housing in the mid-1990s. His current effort to provide housing for low-income families in many areas of the United States is also evidence of this humanist inclination.

In retirement, Rouse founded the Enterprise Development Corporation, a private real estate development firm, which continues to reflect his passion for developing marketplaces in urban communities. One of the most recent is Waterside in Norfolk, Virginia. There are several more on the drawing boards.

Profits from this development corporation are funneled through the Enterprise Foundation, a non-profit, publicly supported foundation begun in 1982. The purpose of this foundation is, according to its 1983 annual report, "to help the very poor help themselves to decent livable housing and out of poverty and dependency into self-sufficiency."

Third, Rouse is an urbanologist. But he is not a theoretical urban sociologist who views the city in a detached and clinical way. He loves and believes in the city; he finds it central to a civilization and is convinced that it makes an indispensable contribution to society. His entire adult life has been one of helping people see the potential for renewal and vitality existing in cities. For Rouse, the city is people. He has often said the only legitimate purpose of a city is to provide for the life and growth of its people.

A natural consequence is the fourth theme dominating Rouse's life and lectures: the festival marketplace. From his first mall in Harundale near Baltimore to such urban gems as Philadelphia's Gallery in Market East to Grand Avenue Mall in Milwaukee, Rouse wanted to bring life, beauty, spirit, and humaneness to the development of places where people shop.

The mutually indispensable relation of a city to the marketplace is seen in a statement Rouse made as he interpreted the meaning of Harborplace, his festival shopping area at the Inner Harbor in downtown Baltimore. It is another version of his "creed" — the dream of a humane urban environment with shopping-as-fun at the center.

"Cities are learning that no matter what else they do at their heart, they cannot become whole without a lively retail core. Offices, hotels, museums, hospitals, universities, each account for a slice of life of the city. But it is in the marketplace that all people come together — rich and poor, old and young, black and white. It is the democratic, unifying, universal place which gives spirit and personality to the city and provides, at its best, the most appealing entertainment available."[3] We can see that the festival marketplace combines the three other themes of dreaming, humanism, and interest in the city.

All of these themes are integral to a complex and sensitive man who is also a successful business person and a philanthropist. But the whole man is more than the sum of his parts. These themes naturally overlap in Rouse's life and are not separated as he goes about his day-to-day decision-making. The urban dreamer is also the humanist seeking to elevate the dignity of people. The multimillionaire is also the man who "dresses down," drives modest cars, and is eager to share his wealth.

But James Rouse can only be understood by knowing his personal background and religious vision. His philosophy of life and business enterprise is fueled by a deep commitment to the values of the Judeo-Christian heritage. This is readily seen by researching his speeches, articles about him, and the products of his development corporation.

Rouse's official vita gives only a bare outline of his life and work. He apparently prefers it that way. The rest of his resume must be fleshed out by consulting people who know him and by reading what people have written about him.

James Rouse was born in Easton on Maryland's eastern shore, April 26, 1914. His family was comfortably middle-class. He was an heir to the traditional American values of parents and grandparents whose moral legacy was informed by nineteenth-century Protestantism. Among those values were going to church, working hard, and being honest.

When Rouse was sixteen, in 1930, both his parents died within a year of each other. This catapulted him into adult responsibility and forced him to mature more rapidly than his peers. It gave him a sense of self-reliance not usually present in most people until later in life.

After attending Tome Institute, a small private academy in Port Deposit, Maryland, Rouse graduated from Easton High School. He then attended — in quick succession — the universities of Hawaii and Virginia. Returning to Baltimore, he enrolled in the University of Maryland's law school. While working odd jobs during the day, he attended classes at night. After graduation from law school in 1937, he was soon admitted to the Maryland Bar.

Between 1937 and 1939 he was employed by the Federal Housing Administration and the Title Guaranty Company. His second job was as a partner in a mortgage banking firm which he helped form and which was the predecessor of the

Rouse Company. From 1942 to 1945, he served in the navy on the staff of Commander Air Force Pacific Fleet. At the end of the war, he was discharged as a lieutenant commander and returned to be chief executive officer of the company he founded. He held this position until his retirement from the Rouse Company in 1979.

He has served on many state and national boards and agencies ranging from the Board of Trustees of The Johns Hopkins University to the American Institute of Landscape Architects. Presidents from Eisenhower to Reagan have recognized his expertise in matters of housing and urban renewal and have appointed him to high-level advisory boards and task forces.

A short while after retiring from the leadership of the Rouse Company, he founded the Enterprise Foundation, the charitable arm of his Enterprise Development Corporation. This venture fulfilled his dream of providing support for low-income people by restoring slum housing to more acceptable and livable conditions.

Rouse's specific interest in assisting the redevelopment of urban housing began in the early 1970s, when he made a substantial financial contribution to inaugurate Jubilee Housing, a non-profit corporation intended to help rehabilitate housing for the very poor in Washington, D.C.

Not coincidentally, Jubilee Housing is a mission outreach of the Church of the Savior, a small Christian community to which Rouse remains actively related. The driving force behind the life, thought, and work of this Mahatma of malls is his faith.

Rouse's 1979 retirement speech to stockholders, along with several others made since, contains the mature reflections of the man on his life's meaning and purpose. These speeches contain valuable clues to what motivated him, what energized him, and the coping mechanisms he used to deal with stress, failure, and frustration.

Toward the end of the retirement speech, he referred to

several symbols in his office that he wanted to pass on to the new chief executive officer, Mathias Devito. The first was a modern translation of the Bible. When he gave it to Devito, he said,

> You may never need to read it, but its presence in your office will stand for the fundamental values that you and I hold high in leading the Company. It is a set of values that says you do not have the responsibility to win — but to give your best, to use your gifts, to respect the dignity of all men and women, to know that as it reaches out and works for the good of mankind, it is right.

In other words — as he has indicated in a dozen other places — Rouse understands the Bible to be a cultural symbol and a source of Western values.

He sees the biblical message as a call for us to be co-creators with God. This view of people, God, and history places him firmly in the camp of liberal Christianity which says "God has no hands but our hands."

Rouse's liberal Christianity emphasizes the goodness of creation, and this definitely includes human beings. Affirmation of the world's goodness implies a minimizing, though not exclusion, of Christ's redemptive work for fallen and sinful humanity. Although people can be selfish and egotistic, they have the capacity and potential to make rational and loving decisions.

This belief in the relative goodness of people, this positive valuation of human nature, enables Rouse to be optimistic and hopeful. It is the source of his amazing ability to become enthusiastic easily, to put the best light on every situation, and to convince others to see through the same optimistic glasses.

Some of Rouse's business associates considered this approach to be naive and to be over selling. But all of this optimism is rooted firmly in his view of God and the world.

Illustrating this further is the framed statement which hangs in the marketing office of White Marsh Mall in Maryland, written by Rouse himself. "Man is God's instrument for carrying out the ongoing creation. That means everything we do in the environment, what we build or fail to build, places a tremendous responsibility on us — and a tremendous opportunity."

In this philosophical-religious statement, as well as in many others, there is an unacknowledged Calvinism — the notion that the Protestant ethic of hard work and success are signs that you are among God's elect.

Rouse is in that long tradition of American businessmen (Carnegie, Rockefeller, and Mellon, to name a few) who were convinced you could be a Christian capitalist and a millionaire. A vocation to commerce, they believed, could be combined with a certain *noblesse oblige*, resulting in concern for the larger society expressed in generosity and philanthropy. Often, along with financially successful careers, these men had uneasy consciences and wondered what they should do with their acquired fortunes and status. Should they not be used to help the less fortunate? Should blessings from God not be shared with others? Rouse, too, grapples with these questions.

He says that a destiny-determining moment for him occurred while attending Brown Memorial Presbyterian Church in Baltimore. While still a young man, Rouse heard the Rev. Guthrie Speers preach about the importance of a concrete relationship between churchgoing and everyday life. The sermon's no-nonsense approach to religion intrigued Rouse. And the lessons of Speers' practical Christianity were not lost on him.

Several years later, a friend told him about the Church of the Savior in Washington, D.C. He suggested Rouse read a book about the church, *Call to Commitment*, by Elizabeth O'Conner. This small ecumenical Christian community was founded by Gordon Cosby soon after World War II and quickly developed a national reputation by insisting on qualitative commitment from its members. Each was to be involved regularly in spiritual disciplines and social service. Members attempted to embody the wholistic message of Christianity by balancing the inward and outward journeys of faith.

Rouse joined the church in the early 1960s and spent four years in a school for Christian living sponsored by the church and taught by the Rev. Cosby. The school concentrated on theology and ethics. The text studied in some depth during the course was theologian Paul Jones' *Recovery of Life's Meaning.* It was part of the popular theology prevalent twenty years ago. It had a profound impact on Rouse and he refers to it again and again in his speeches.

This book spelled out the idea of people as co-creators with God. Years later, Rouse recalled that Jones spoke of the theology of co-creativity between people and God, a theology which finds creation not an event in the past, but a continuing process; it finds us in a covenant relationship to work with God to carry forward the process of creation. Thus, we proceed in trustful dependence upon God's purpose and power; we are instruments on earth to sustain God's creation.

On another occasion, Rouse commented on the same book: "We are co-creators with God . . . in what happens to the natural environment, what happens to the institutions we create, and what happens to our individual relationship with mankind."[4]

Jones' work was a simplified version — almost a layman's version — of a theological emphasis widespread in the 1960s. At a more sophisticated level, it was represented by Harvey Cox's *God's Revolution and Man's Responsibility* and his more famous *The Secular City.* Much of this so-called secular theology finally relied on the highly theoretical work of Frederich Gogarten's *Der Mensch Zwischen Gott und Welt* (*Man Between God and World*). The fundamental thesis of this position was that God has turned the world over to us as our responsibility, and that we are accountable to God for our stewardship.

Following this course, Rouse began to ask seriously, "How

can I be a faithful Christian? What is my responsibility in the world? How can I best use my talent, time, and treasure to the glory of God?" As a result of these reflections, he adopted the model of the Church of the Savior's inner and outward journey dialectic. Spirituality is tested by one's attempt to make the world a more humane place. Rouse saw a direct line from Guthrie Speers' sermon to Jones' theology of co-creatorship, to ameliorating the plight of our cities' poor.

God's vision for the city, a God-centered urban community, is, to paraphrase Rouse, one of beauty, well-being, people in creative support for one another, and the functioning of love. It is not "the violence and suffocation of the human spirit and the hopelessness that pervades the American city."[5]

When Rouse sees the distance between the city of God and the modern city, he does not despair. He sees the modern city rather as a challenge. Let us learn from the past, he says, not lament it. Indeed, this leads to the second symbol Rouse gave Devito at that retirement dinner. It was a slogan hanging on Rouse's office wall: "When life gives you lemons, make lemonade."

This irrepressible buoyancy is rooted firmly in Rouse's conviction that we are partners with God, helping God's work in the world: renewing, re-creating, revitalizing, restoring, making human life richer and fuller. We do not bring God to the world. It is our duty to share God's work, which is already in progress. "Our mission," says Rouse, "is to be at work with our gifts, our resources, and our relationships — inventing, moving, trying, failing, learning, creating — not wringing our hands and wailing about the past, about the failures of government, about the corruption of politicians and landlords, about the greed of the rich, or the infinite frustration that impedes what we see as rational progress."

In Rouse's view of life, there is no real adversity. There are only events in which we are responsible for finding a creative potential. There is always another side to adversity. Enemies become potential friends. Failures are new beginnings. Lemons become lemonade. Making lemonade, in other words, is to view the gap between God's purpose and our performance not as destiny, but as malfunction; not as failure, but as challenge, opportunity, and hope.

Rouse needed this unbounded optimism and confidence to see the possibility of new humanity in the decaying American city of the 1950s and 1960s. To kindle his optimism, Rouse often recalled this quote from Dietrich Bonhoeffer, a German pastor imprisoned by Hitler. In one of his prison letters, he wrote,

> In its essence, optimism is not a view of the present situation, but a strength for life, a strength of hope where others are resigned, strength to hold one's head up when everything seems to go wrong, power to bear setbacks, strength that never leaves the future to the opponent, but lays claim to it for oneself.

That Rouse appreciated this assertion from a Christian martyr is clear from the number of times it appears in his speeches. And that he quotes Bonhoeffer, rather than Norman Vincent Peale's "power of positive thinking" or Robert Schuller's "power of possibility thinking" — both concepts from popular public religious figures to which he had access — indicates he is more sensitive than most Christian laity to the realism of Christian confidence about people and history.

The last symbol Rouse bequeathed to Devito at that retirement celebration was a quotation found on his desk. It is also a reference you find throughout Rouse's lectures, especially in the more personal and autobiographical. The lines are from Daniel Burnham, a Chicago businessman of a generation ago:

> "Make no little plans, they have no magic to stir men's blood and probably themselves will not be realized. Make big plans; aim high in hope and work, remembering that a noble logical diagram once recorded will never die, but long after we are gone will be a living thing, asserting itself with ever-growing insistency. Remember that our sons and grandsons are going to do things that would stagger us."[6]

It is interesting to see the recurrence of this theme in the titles of his speeches during the past several years:

"Places That Make a Difference," May 1977

"Utopia: Limited or Unlimited," November 1979

"Make No Little Plans," November 1983

In James Rouse, we have a person who understands both the practicality of dreaming and the need to envision the future.

In the author's view, there are two significant reasons why dreaming is necessary and practical. First, if a dream is a good one, such as the biblical one of the Messianic Era or the Kingdom of God or the Christian one of the City of God, it has the power to attract us to its fulfillment. There is a magnetic quality about such a dream. No satisfaction is possible until the vision is materialized. Response to such a vision empowers people to realize that dream in history. The visionary's determination to fulfill the dream invariably involves him or her with the establishment. This was true of James Rouse, who had to fight for a long time to get his malls and marketplaces as people centers accepted by the "powers that be."

Second, if a dream is a good one, it is always standing in judgment on our historical approximation of it. This is important because it insures us against thinking we have fully realized our dream. The dream always exceeds our grasp and will always be in the process of completion. Or, to use Rouse's words: "The power of the large image [is] the power of the ideal that reaches beyond what we think we can do."

It is impossible to understand Rouse apart from this religious vision of God or power and the human beings' capacity to share that creative power in remaking the world. The direction that energy led Rouse was to renew the American city by humanly commercial centers and festival marketplaces.

Mildred F. Schmirtz, writing in the *Architectural Record* (December 1977), said Rouse somehow has never forgotten that shopping and eating should be a pleasure as well as a necessity and they would be just that in a place "where people could walk for fun, where they could relax, eat, browse, and buy." His success has been in realizing that memory.

Rouse sees all positive activity as participation in the work of God. To co-create with God is also to re-create (recreation). It is natural for Rouse to see festive human interaction as inspired by and responding to God.

Rouse would understand the early church father Ireneaus' remark: "The glory of God is a fully human life." Nothing is clearer for Rouse than that religion should be a humanizing force in the world. His liberal impulses led him to restate Ireneaus' observation in a secular way: "I believe that the ultimate test of civilization is whether or not it contributes to the growth and improvement of mankind. Does it uplift, inspire, stimulate, and develop the best in man?"[7]

Perhaps the best summary of Rouse's philosophy and religious vocation is a quote to a newspaper reporter almost a decade ago. "The only real purpose and justification of any one of these centers is to serve the people in the area — not the merchants, not the architects, not the developers. The success or failure of a regional shopping center will be measured by what it does for the people it seeks to serve."[8] Or to put it more succinctly, will festival marketplaces and shopping centers pass this ultimate Rouse test: "Do they grow people?"

Many of the personal traits of this Mahatma of malls — commitment, risk-taking, optimism, humaneness, trust in people — are found in a couplet from Goethe which Rouse quoted to conclude one of his major speeches:

What ever you can do, or dream you can, do it;
Boldness has genius, power and magic in it.

Few would question that the centers of human renewal he has designed — from regional shopping malls to festival marketplaces to his latest endeavor in low-income housing — have boldness, genius, and magic.

· 4 ·

Mall as Sacred Time

Johan Huizinga, the Dutch historian of culture, has said, "The play-mood is one of rapture and enthusiasm, and is sacred or festive in accordance with the occasion."[1] While shopping malls are not carbon copies of New Year's Eve, Mardi Gras, or Octoberfest, a definite air of festivity and frolic may be found in them. Their atmosphere resembles a combination carnival midway and resort boardwalk. Some have compared the flavor of malls to a form of Disneyland. One does find the gaiety and abandon of an amusement park, especially at certain seasons of the year. The total impact of color, music, smell, and entertaining sounds is inescapable and inviting.

Festival Marketplace

Mall promoters and their advertisements, without hesitation, use such language as "shopping as fun," "Festival Marketplace" (James Rouse), and "recreational retailing" (Robert Brindle), as ways to describe the appeal of the mall experience. One recent article in *The Baltimore Sun Magazine* devoted a good deal of space to malls under the title "The Allure of Shopping" and quoted Scott Ditch, vice-president for corporate-public affairs for the Rouse Company. He said "(Our) shopping centers are patterned after ancient European marketplaces, where meat vendors and jugglers worked side by side."[2]

James Rouse himself summarizes this aspect of the mall

FANEUIL HALL MARKETPLACE, *Boston*
Mimes, jugglers, and magicians perform for a crowd. The carnival atmosphere provided here is integral to the popularity of malls. Courtesy, Rouse Co.

when he says that "shopping is increasingly entertainment
and a competitor with other entertainment choices. In a cir-
cumstance of delight, it gratifies a need that might otherwise
be met by a trip to New York, or a weekend at the beach."[3]

In fact, nothing illustrates better the "more than" nature of
the contemporary mall than the invitations you find in many
public relations brochures distributed by mall offices. This
"more than" means that the mall is not only a convenient and
well-functioning place of business; it is also a good and entertaining place.

A few examples:

> "Meet me at White Flint for Fun, Fashion, Dining, Shopping, and a
> Great Day."

> "The People ride the buses, take the subways, walk the streets of the
> city to the center of celebration at the Gallery."

> "We're a new kind of country. You can dress it up, size it up, serve it
> up, charm it up, play it up. We do it right."

> "It's in the variety, of course. Century City Shopping Center gives
> you the world. You'll discover the singing flowerman and jelly beans
> in a jar."

Even the names of shops in the mall have a sense of levity
and playfulness about them. Apart from the established family
names of the chain department stores that serve as anchors,
you find shops and stores almost making light of themselves
with their names. Many of these small shops also belong to national chains and are frequently found in the shopping malls.

Body Talk, The Underworld, Up's and Down's, Figure Fair,
and Hit or Miss are examples of names for stores dealing with
women's apparel. Men who are interested in shopping for
clothing will discover Pants' Pocket, Denim Den, Chess King,
and His Store. The Wild Pair, Bootlegger, Athlete's Foot,
and Footlocker are names of shoe stores while such signs as

Keep in Touch, Mac the Knife, Wicks and Sticks, Tees for Two, and In the Bag hang above specialty gift shops.

Businesses specializing in gourmet food are known as Chez Frommage, The Candy Bar, and A La Mode. Finally, those shops which concentrate in personal care and services go by such catchy handles as Your Father's Mustache and Tender Sender. And on it goes. There is a party-like, low-threat, delightful quality to these names. They contribute to fun and fantasy and the relaxed environment of the mall.

Even granted the seductive nature of the language, the average person does not conclude that the mall's intention is to manipulate and to exploit us. Festivity is more than the mall's urge to accommodate. In many cases, it itself is the main event in the center ring.

Nature of Play

Both Johan Huizinga and Roger Callois have affirmed that a spirit of play is essential to a culture. Callois has written one of the most important studies on the place of play in human experience. His book, *Man, Play, and Games*, contains two broad categories of play. The first is *paidia* — childlike activity characterized by freedom, spontaneity, carefree gaiety, and impersonation. The second is *ludens* — play usually associated with games involving rules, order, and boundaries. These two basic categories provide a framework for his fourfold typology of play: *agon* (competition), *alea* (chance), *mime* (simulation), and *ilinx* (vertigo).

Festivity in the malls and *paidia* seem naturally aligned with each other, since the two aspects of play most frequently seen and enacted at the malls are simulation and vertigo. Simulation is present in the many theatrical and dramatic performances sponsored by malls. Clowns, puppets, Santa Claus, the Easter Bunny and other disguised characters are all present.

As spectators on the one hand, we have a fascination for

mime and impersonation, and, on the other hand, we desire to imitate, suspend rules, and poke fun. If you have ever been to a carnival or fiesta, you remember this sort of playing, pantomime and simulation abound. We are caught up in it and often participate vicariously in it.

Secondly, vertigo is illustrated explicitly by such activities as whirling, dancing, and swinging. The classic form of this type of play is expressed in the riding of Ferris wheels, roller coasters, carousels, as well as climbing mountains, and walking tightropes. Without these events (with the possible exception of the carousel), the mall does create for us what Callois sees as vertigo. It attempts to "momentarily destroy the stability of perception and inflict a kind of voluptuous panic upon our otherwise lucid mind. In all cases, it is a question of surrendering to a kind of spasm, seizure, or shock which destroys reality with sovereign brusqueness."[4]

This is the experience we had as children when we first entered a carnival, or when we emerged from a hallway onto a steep theater balcony, or climbed to the highest tier of bleachers in an athletic stadium. In a similar vein, the mall can create a certain vertigo with its cacophany of sound, blurred sights, splashes of color, and multiplicity of smells; all of these are combined with the illusion of vast space. It is a fascinating feeling. We are both attracted and repelled; we want to continue on and we wish to withdraw — like our apprehension about looking down on the mall's center court from our perch four stories above in a glass-enclosed elevator. One thing is certain: our response is never lukewarm or neutral.

It is often an overwhelming experience. But eventually we adjust and in the end enjoy the play, pageantry, and magic. After a bit of intoxication and ecstasy, we begin to focus and put the excitement around us into perspective. This enables us to survive and to handle the experience with relative success.

Both of these diversions, mimicry and vertigo, offer an alternative to the boredom, monotony, and fatalism which are part of so many lives. Many people go to the mall for the fun of it, for a break in the routine of their serious, well-regulated world. In the mall they are part of another time, even though they, themselves, may not be participating in any way.

This reminds me of a poster advertising a college fraternity party. After the event's time and place were stated, there was the phrase "Escape with us to a different time." This sacred time, this discontinuous, qualitatively different time, affords us a "break," "time out," an interruption in the normal, day-to-day routine of our nine-to-five lives. It is in this religious time that play and ritual occur.

Play has an almost universal religious reference. David Miller, in *Gods and Games: Toward A Theology of Play*, reminds us that children, Jesus, and ancient religious traditions remember what theologians have forgotten. "The Kingdom of God is a kingdom of play; unless you receive the Kingdom of God as a child, you cannot enter it."[5]

This is a Christian version of the old Hindu idea that God's activity is a form of sport or play (*lila*), an activity which is free, spontaneous, and done for its own sake. This is reflected in one of the most famous symbols of the world's religions, the dancing Shiva. The implication is that God dances the creation and the world is the dance of God.

A contemporary sociologist of religion, Peter Berger, helps us see that play is a rumor or hint of the transcendent. In his book *Rumors of Angels*, Berger says that, among other human experiences, play is a signal of the supernatural, of a reality beyond, of the angelic. Berger says that in play we find a sense of freedom and joy because, in playing, "one steps out of one time into another — out of the dying chronology of ordinary time into an eternal moment." For example, the citizens of the little Jewish community of Anatevka, fictionalized in *Fiddler on the Roof* by Sholom Aleichem, danced at a wedding in the presence of Russian persecution, and, by doing so, pointed themselves and us toward a reality which transcends their sometimes-tormented everyday time.

The festive nature of the shopping mall makes a similar

statement. A mall's playful atmosphere points us beyond commerce, barter, and trade. Playing in the mall tells us that life is not finally lived at the level of monetary transactions, and that such exchanges will take place in an atmosphere of fun and conviviality. Festivity in the mall is a not-so-subtle subversion of the marketplace and the serious, hard-working, profit-making entrepreneur. It is a protest of the mall's potential to deceive and to manipulate. We counter charade with charade. Play in the mall reminds customers that there exists in the citadel of capitalism another bottom line besides the profit-margin, namely, jest and comedy. The actual presence of jesters and clowns in our malls is an embodiment of the whole sense of carnival and fiesta found in them. Like medieval court jesters, they mock, tease, and otherwise remind the emperor that he has no clothes. The play element in mall culture seems to be a way of saying that we will not take the commercial enterprise with ultimate seriousness; we will provide a safety valve, a release, a diversion. Perhaps it also means that we will not take seriously our yielding to the come-ons of marketing specialists. In any case, the mall serves effectively as one of these moments of distractions.

Types of Play

UNORGANIZED PLAY

Obviously what I am about to describe does not "just happen." The mall makes available space and opportunity in the forms of conference rooms, free space around the center, and staging areas for some serendipitous experiences to occur and also allows the visitor to plan his or her activities. In any case, the organization of this activity is up to us.

It is interesting to see that the mall has responded to the jogging craze. Some malls have mapped out one-to-five-mile courses in their parking lots and publicized them for local runners. The runners are usually permitted to jog in the early

morning, before the stores open. Older people desiring regular exercise will use the inside of the mall as a place to walk for
a few miles without worry about weather or safety. Willow
Brook Mall in Wayne, New Jersey has a measured course
within the mall itself for senior citizens interested in briefer,
but regular, periods of exercise.

Some malls have play areas for children, combined with
babysitting services. These are usually found near the center,
where there are also frequently found large stationary wooden
animals for children to climb on and pretend to ride. There is
an increasing sensitivity to the need for children to play freely
and spontaneously. Of a piece with all this is the frequency
with which you find wandering clowns with balloons, strolling
minstrels, and puppet shows. In season, Santa Claus, the
Great Pumpkin (with accompanying pumpkin-judging contests), and the Easter Bunny are all on hand. And, of course,
your picture can be taken with any of these special visitors.

At White Marsh Mall near Baltimore, the arrival of Santa
with bags of goodies is a main event inaugurating the Christmas season. Children meet the "real Santa Claus" in a specially
designed Nutcracker Sweet Village. We are told the kids will
enjoy "Santa's Nutcracker Express," train rides in Hutzler's
Court, and "The Sugarplum Sweet Carousel" in Pic-Nic and
much more.

There is, however, a form of play I am constrained to mention which is different from mime and vertigo. It is *agon*, e.g.
ordeal, struggle, competition. This "game" begins when you
have completed your visit to the mall and are ready to return
to your car in the parking lot. If you do not recall that you
parked in Lot A, Section 16, you may be playing what I call
"mall hopscotch." Callois suggests that the children's game of
hopscotch is rooted in archaic societies' initiation rites. Before
being admitted into adult status, an initiate had to wander
successfully through a complicated labyrinth.

I once was caught in one of these primordial mazes when I

exited a mall opposite where my car was parked. Since the exterior of this particular mall was uniform in appearance, with no differentiation between front or back, east or west, I thought I was in the general area of my parked car. After half an hour of futile searching, I told a young man my plight. He asked me what road I entered the mall on. I told him. "Oh," he said, "you belong on the other side of the mall. Get in my car, and I will take you over there." It would have been a long afternoon without that bit of advice. Agony, indeed!

PERFORMANCES

These typically occur at the center, where there is either a permanent stage or a temporary platform for actors and musicians. Some malls provide a miniature amphitheater with two or three levels for spectators.

What happens here depends to a large extent on the time of year, the neighboring community, and the artistic tastes of most consumers. Concerts are usually held on Saturdays, or perhaps Thursday and Friday nights. Jazz bands, rock groups, country singers, square dancers, and clog dancing are ordinary fare. An audience will gather to watch and listen as time permits. Since the crowd of onlookers converge at the center, the prestige of the center as a place of festive human interaction is reinforced. Shop owners are willing to pay higher rental fees for this coveted location.

A variety of performing groups will entertain from this same spot during the Christmas season. As said earlier, no season attracts more community groups and traveling shows than Christmas time. For instance, at Baltimore's White Marsh Mall during thirty or more shopping days between Thanksgiving and Christmas in 1983, there were three performances of *The Nutcracker* by the Metropolitan Ballet and over thirty concerts by nearby elementary, middle, and high school bands and choruses, as well as by several concert choirs from community churches. On most days there were two performances, one midday and one in early evening.

Pantomimes, puppet shows, and modern dance performances are also staged in this area. These activities are carefully orchestrated and designed to attract people to the mall and to entertain them while they are there.

The staging of ethnic festivals is another significant aspect of the mall's inclination to meet community needs and to inform and entertain. Such festivals are particularly popular on the east coast from New England to Florida. They are small versions of what Baltimore does so successfully throughout the summer around its Inner Harbor.

I visited Long Island's Smith Haven Mall during Greek Festival Week. The center amphitheater provided the excitement and gaiety of Greek folk dancing accompanied by a Greek band and chorus. By circling the stage, you could find booths selling mousaka, baklava, and other Greek food, books on Greek culture and history, and handcrafted pottery, woolen sweaters, and jewelry. This sort of multi-media event is replicated in as many different ways as there are ethnic organizations interested in sponsoring them. The malls can enhance ethnic pride and dignity while providing unique entertainment. Mall public events coordinators are responsive to America's ethnic pluralism, not its reputation as a melting pot. And this list does not begin to exhaust the kinds of performers you can find at a mall.

COMMERCIAL ENTERTAINMENT

There is, of course, ample opportunity to pay for play. Malls have kept abreast of the youth culture's demand for electronic games. In addition, a plethora of pinball machines fill the penny arcades. Such commercial play remains a strong drawing card for the teen culture.

Some malls feature large, carnival-sized carousels. The manager of White Marsh Mall thought it would be a good idea to have a merry-go-round for the Christmas season; it was so popular it became a permanent fixture. Smaller, coin-operated carousels with only four animals, are frequently found. In a few malls, you can find small trains for children to ride; they are similar to those you would see at a small carnival or amusement park.

And there is virtually an endless variety of other coin-operated entertainments, from the simple hobby horse to airplanes to stage coaches. Children can also stand near The Little Castle and listen through a telephone to stories about beasts, witches, and fairies. The "run-your-own-train-set" is a relatively new phenomenon. For a quarter, children of all ages can direct an oversized model train around an elaborate course running through miniature mountains and tunnels, over streams, and next to small villages. The entire set is encased in a large glass display case.

Then there are the usual booths which, for a price, take your picture, and the scales which weigh you and tell your fortune.

Because the mall has the power to draw crowds, movie theater chains quickly seized the opportunity to open local theaters. You can often find theaters with two to six small auditoriums showing a range of films, rated from G to R.

Several malls I visited featured a relatively new expression of play—ice skating rinks. These rinks, in effect, become the center court. You pay an admission fee and rent skates by the hour. A rink manager in Florida told me that the obvious reason for this form of entertainment was to attract customers. Among other reasons is the significant one of satisfying the nostalgia of northerners who have migrated to the Sunbelt.

In addition, there are other organized activities and exercise classes which charge admission fees. These range from aerobic classes to dance studios specializing in ballet, modern dance, and tap. High schools have even held senior proms in the community rooms of some larger malls.

The traditional strip shopping center, limited to small coin-operated machines in front of a store or two, could not supply such a variety of entertainment. The mall alone has the capacity and the desire to provide this festival and carnival atmosphere.

Ceremonial Center

"There is always something going on here," said a woman in a New Jersey mall. What goes on there is most easily understood in terms of ritual and ceremony. Those words, ritual and ceremony, have similar derivations. Ritual is rooted in the Sanskrit, *Rta* (from which we get *ritus* and rite), a cosmic force which keeps the world turning at its proper pace. *Rta* guarantees order and regularity to the seasons and human life. Ceremony is from *Ceres*, the Roman goddess of agriculture, who could be counted on annually to guarantee fertility and produce crops (cereal!).

Both *Rta* and *Ceres* suggest that ritual and ceremony have an annual reference, i.e., a reference to harvest festivals and the renewal of the year. Malls, along with other human communities, respond to this natural urge to recognize and help celebrate national holidays, traditional religious holidays, and social days. In addition, malls have their own special commercial celebrations from month to month throughout the year.

There is always a communal base to ritual. It takes place within some form of community, whether it be tribe, family, village, or nation. Ritual loses its meaning when performed in isolation. Can you imagine celebrating your birthday alone? Food courts flourish in our malls because eating alone has become a bane of our culture. Any experience, including experiencing the mall, is totally different in solitude than in the company of others.

And it is by way of ritual that a community defines itself and remembers who it is. Its identity is linked to certain meaningful events it decides to celebrate regularly. The mall acts as a ceremonial center responsive not only to the needs of financial solvency, but to the psychic, social, religious, and patriotic needs so easily felt in all of us.

These rituals and seasonal celebrations help maintain harmony between the mall and the surrounding community. They express the symbiotic relationship many malls experience with their wider constituency. Ceremony at the center keeps lines of communication open and periodically reminds the community that the mall is not a threatening and intimidating place. The original purpose of ritual was to maintain peace and reconciliation between gods and people, to foster a parallelism of the divine and human worlds. The ceremonial activity in the malls, with its ability to preserve continuity between center and periphery, helps the patron retain a conscious sense of connection to what is happening in the mall.

In addition, there is similarity and repetition in ritual expression. It is always the same thing, done in the same prescribed manner, on the same day, weekly or annually. This is what makes it ritual. The repetitive character of ritual gives us a sense of security in the world. Ritual and ceremony inform us that we can count on life and history continuing with some meaning. Just as we know generally what will take place in church, synagogue, Rotary Club gathering, or 4-H meeting, so we know what will take place in a mall. It is this familiarity, reinforced by ritual, which finally prevents the mall from overwhelming us. As the old Chinese proverb goes "rites obviate disorder as dikes prevent inundation."[6]

Human communities, be they sororities, families, religious organizations, or sporting events, ritualize, unfailingly, their activities. And malls are no exception.

The average mall definitely orders its year and its ceremonial life reflects the holidays and seasons of the year. The annual cycle of the mall's events is highlighted by recognizing national observances, traditional religious holidays, personal and family celebrations, and other rhythms of the year. In between these activities are regularly scheduled business specials, sales days, and commercial promotions. These events are carefully planned, often months or a year in advance. And all the shop and store owners are assessed a percentage to help sponsor them.

The mall's ritual and ceremonial life ensures that the year will continue to flow with facility, will be complete, and will eventually be reborn.

Here is what the liturgical year or annual directory of events looks like for the average mall:

National Observances		Religious Holidays	
January	Martin Luther King's birthday	April	Easter (Easter Bunny)
February	Presidents' birthdays		Passover
July	Independence Day	December	Christmas (Santa Claus)
September	Labor Day		Hanukkah
November	Thanksgiving		

Personal and Family Celebrations		Business Promotions	
February	Valentine's Day	January	"Sidewalk Sales"
May	Mother's Day	March	Spring Sales Days
June	Father's Day	June	Gift Days
September	Grandparents' Day		Weddings
October	Halloween (Great Pumpkin)		Commencements
		August	Pre-school Sales
		October	Homebuilder's Month
			Furniture Sales

Once or twice during the year, usually in January or August, there will be "moonlight madness" sales for the venturesome and the "lunatics." Every month has at least one major business emphasis or promotion. And so the year moves along.

The following statement, sent to all the merchants at Crossroads Mall in Boulder, Colorado, indicates how the proposed schedule of activities can be integrated for the year.

MEMORANDUM

To: Crossroads Mall Merchants Association
Store Managers and Store Owners

From: Jean Redmond, Marketing Director

Subject: Crossroads Mall Store Directory
Special Advertising Sections
1984 Calendar of Events

Scott W. Burchard
Asst. Vice President
Regional Manager

James W. Swenson
Assistant Manager

Jean Redmond
Marketing Director

Karen Joiner
Marketing Assistant

The information in this booklet is provided to assist you in coordinating your advertising and promotional efforts with those of Crossroads Mall.

We have outlined the cooperative advertising sections, the major promotions, and a number of community events, however, as we go forward into 1984 we will be adding to this schedule of events. You will be informed of these additions (i.e. auto shows, boat shows, etc.) through a monthly newsletter which will be implemented as of March, 1984.

I look forward to working closely with all of you to achieve our mutual goals of making Crossroads Mall the number one shopping choice in this region and one of the most integral parts of our community.

Please feel free to contact me at anytime if I can be of service to you.

HERE'S TO AN EXCELLENT, SUCCESSFUL 1984!

CROSSROADS MALL

CROSSROADS BUSINESS OFFICE 1600-28TH BOULDER, COLORADO 80301 303/444-0722

Alternating with these commercial, religious, and national festivals, are periodic scheduled events such as fashion shows, flea markets, antique shows, boat exhibits, auto shows, fine arts displays, fencing tournaments, and flower marts. Some of these can become extravaganzas and have in some malls developed national reputations like the Easter Eggsibition sponsored by the Dallas Society for Crippled Children (an Easter Seal Affiliate) in the Galleria. One hundred and twenty-five ostrich eggs are hand-decorated by amateur artists and displayed for customers and visitors.

With this sort of careful event planning, it is not difficult to book events a year or so in advance. The merchants — as well as community groups including churches, schools, and entertainers of all kinds — have ample time to respond.

Here are some illustrations of how market managers plan meticulously for their monthly and yearly activities:

JANUARY 1984

**15	Super Sunday
	1 Day Sale Event
*20–22	Computer Show

FEBRUARY 1984

*2–5	Historic Boulder Antique Show
*16–20	President's Portrait Display

Community Events

1. February 8 & 11 — U.S. Army Display
2. February 10–14 — Let Me Call You Sweetheart —
   Free Phone Call Promotion
3. February 25–26 — Boulder Valley Youth
   Hockey Fund Raising

Community Events

1. March 3-4 — Boulder Valley Schools— Student Art Exhibit
2. March 3 — McDonald's Benefit Breakfast for Boulder Valley Youth Hockey
3. March 4 & 24 — Civil Air Patrol Information Booth
4. March 5-11 — Colorado Music Festival Antique Car Raffle
5. March 11-17 — National Surveyors Week Display and Information Booth
6. March 17 — Campfire Girls and Boys Birthday Week Fair
7. March 31 — Timberline Chorus Performance

APRIL 1984

*7-11   Red Cross Health Fair
*14   YWCA Wine & Cheese Tasting Benefit
*18-21   Easter Story Hour

Community Events

1. April 7-8, 14-15 — Boulder Philharmonic Fund Raising Promotion
2. April 18-21 — Arbor Day Student Art Exhibit

A monthly calendar for Crossroads Mall in Boulder, Colorado.

CHRISTMAS CONCERT SERIES

Sunday, December 1	3pm	Metropolitan Ballet
Monday,	11am	Norwood Berkshire Chorus
December 2	7pm	PentaBrass Quintet
Tuesday,	12:30pm	Perry Hall Middle School
December 3	7pm	Joppatowne High Chorus
Wednesday,	11:30am	Parkville Middle School Band
December 4	7pm	Patapsco High Band

Thursday, December 5	1pm	Deep Creek 8th grade Chorus & Band
	7pm	St. Mark Choir & Folk Ensemble
Friday, December 6	1pm	Deep Creek 7th grade Chorus & Band
	7pm	Gospel Tabernacle Choir
Saturday, December 7	7pm	Metropolitan Dance
Sunday, December 8	3pm	Parkville High Band
Monday, December 9	1pm	St. Paul's Junior Choir
	7pm	Catholic High Band
Tuesday, December 10	1pm	GlenMar Elementary Choir
	7pm	Kenwood High Chorus & Band
Wednesday, December 11	1pm	Deep Creek 6th grade Chorus & Band
	7pm	North Carroll High School
Thursday, December 12	1pm	Hereford Middle Chorus
	7pm	Edgewood Choir
Friday, December 13	1pm	Sparrows Point Chorus
	7pm	American Legion
Saturday, December 14	1pm	John Leon Lewis
	7pm	Metropolitan Dance
Sunday, December 15	3pm	Metropolitan Dance
Monday, December 16	11:30am	General Stricker
	1pm	Sussex Elementary Choir
	7pm	Parkville High School Chorus
Tuesday, December 17	1pm	Perry Hall Elementary
	7pm	North Harford High Chorus
Wednesday, December 18	11am	Harford Hills Elementary
	1pm	Chesapeake High Chorus & Band
	7pm	Notre Dame Glee Club
Thursday, December 19	11am	Parkville Middle Chorus
	7pm	Inverness Presbyterian Church
Friday, December 20	12:15pm	Parkville High Band
	7pm	Social Security Singers
Saturday, December 21	1pm	Gilman Traveling Men
	7pm	Metropolitan Dance
Sunday, December 22	3pm	St. Joseph Church Choir
	7pm	Hazelwood Baptist Church

The daily schedule of events for White Marsh Mall during an average Christmas season.

LENOX SQUARE

1985 Calendar of Events

JANUARY
  1 New Year's Day
  7 Julian Calendar Christmas
15 Martin Luther King Birthday
26 Fine Arts Show
    through Feb. 3

FEBRUARY
  1–3 Fine Arts Show
12 Lincoln's Birthday
14 St. Valentine's Day
15–20 Belgian/American Week
18 Washington's Birthday observed
20 Ash Wednesday
22 Washington's Birthday
22–24 WGST-Atlanta Symphony Radiothon

MARCH
  1 Spring Fashion Show
4–8 Napps School Display
9–17 Arts & Crafts Show
17 St. Patrick's Day
20 First Day of Spring
23 Easter Bunny Arrives
31 Palm Sunday

APRIL
  5 Good Friday
  6 Passover
  7 Easter Sunday
12 Eastern Orthodox Holy Friday
14 Eastern Orthodox Easter
24 Secretaries' Day

MAY
3–4 Educational Fair
12 Mother's Day
18 Armed Forces Day
18–19 Bonsai Exhibit
27 Memorial Day

JUNE	14 Flag Day
	16 Father's Day
	21 First Day of Summer
	24–30 Stay and See Georgia Week
JULY	4 Independence Day
	Peachtree Road Race & Fireworks
	27–August 4 Watercolor Show
AUGUST	1–4 Watercolor Show
SEPTEMBER	2 Labor Day
	8 Grandparents Day
	16 Rosh Hashanah
	17 Citizenship Day
	22 First Day of Autumn
	25 Yom Kippur
OCTOBER	5 Jaguar Day
	14 Columbus Day
	16 Bosses' Day
	18–24 New Car Show
	19 Sweetest Day
	24 United Nation's Day
	25–28 Wildlife Art Show
	27 Mother-in-Laws' Day
	31 Halloween
NOVEMBER	5 Election Day
	11 Veteran's Day
	23 Santa Arrives
	28 Thanksgiving
DECEMBER	2–24 Holiday Music Programs
	8 Hanukkah
	21 First Day of Winter
	25 Christmas Day

Submitted by:

PENELOPE M. HEATH
Marketing Assistant
Lenox Square Merchants Association, Inc.

The "liturgical" year for Lenox Square in Atlanta. This yearly calendar of events includes business, family, national, and religious holy days.

HALLOWEEN FUN!

IT WILL BE AN EVENING FULL OF FUN AND EXCITEMENT WHEN NORDSTROM MALL HOSTS THEIR ANNUAL HALLOWEEN PROMOTION!

THE FUN ALL STARTS WITH A HALLOWEEN COLORING CONTEST. PRIZES WILL BE AWARDED TO THE FOLLOWING AGE GROUPS: 5 AND UNDER, 6 TO 8, AND 9 TO 12 YEARS. CONTEST FORMS CAN BE PICKED UP FROM ANY NORDSTROM MALL MERCHANT BEGINNING MONDAY, OCTOBER 14TH. ENTRIES MUST BE RETURNED BY: OCTOBER 29TH. WINNERS WILL BE ANNOUNCED OCTOBER 31ST / 6:30 PM.

ENJOY A SAFE, WARM + DRY HALLOWEEN EVENING WITH TRICK-or-TREATING IN ALL 45 STORES FROM 5P.M. TO 6P.M. (WHILE CANDY SUPPLIES LAST)

CAPTURE HALLOWEEN MEMORIES WITH A FREE 5x7 COLOR PICTURE OF YOUR CHILD IN COSTUME, COURTESY OF KITS CAMERAS. PICTURES WILL BE TAKEN FROM 5P.M. TO 9P.M., OCTOBER 31ST.

WHETHER YOU'RE YOUNG OR JUST YOUNG AT HEART... EVERYONE WILL BE ENTERTAINED AND INTRIGUED BY THE FAMILY MAGIC AND ILLUSION OF MARK COLLINS MAGIC SHOWS. FROM A FLOATING LADY TO RABBITS OUT OF A HAT, YOU'RE SURE TO BE MYSTIFIED AND AMAZED! MAGIC SHOWS WILL BE AT 4, 6+7 P.M.

HALLOWEEN FUN AT NORDSTROM MALL!
OCTOBER 31, 1985

nordstrom mall

Nordstrom Mall in Salem, Oregon, represents an increasing number of malls which are having special celebrations at Halloween. Some malls call it Mall-oween.

In response to questions about the rationale for the yearly schedule of events, Kay Muse, Advertising Marketing Director at the Mall in Columbia, Maryland, said, "The promotional events for the year are defined by the marketing area. We will reflect the needs and interests of the community. For example, in some places Martin Luther King, Jr.'s birthday will be a bigger event than in others. The response to ethnic and religious holidays varies with the region."

Proper adherence to such timetables and due acknowledgement of these many "holy days" means that the year is complete, rounded out — the wheel has turned full circle again and with few exceptions the same cycle of programs and ceremonies will begin again in January.

So the mall represents the sacredness of time — business in the context of revelry and party, shopping as escape. The mall is one vast public theater in which we are alternately spectators and performers. Malls as festival marketplaces have brought new life to many places, especially decaying urban areas, and our visits to them may result in our own revitalization.

Ceremonial Meal

The most popular place in a mall, with the possible exception of the center court at show time, is the food court. Here you can find anything from tacos to Chick-fil-A to gourmet restaurants and filet mignon. Jane Thompson, wife and partner of Ben Thompson, a leading architect for The Rouse Company, suggests why food has such universal appeal. She observes that "next to sun and fire, food is our most potent symbol of the life-sustaining forces, offering the warmth, protection, and nurturing that we need. A display of food gives pleasure and reassurance. Food is ritualized in connection with every known holiday."[7]

There is a sense in which every meal is a religious, if not sacramental, act. A prayer before meals is a way of saying, "We will take out time to acknowledge with gratitude that all life comes to us from beyond ourselves." It is not accidental that in the major western religions, Judaism and Christianity, two of the main celebrations center around a meal — Passover and the Eucharist. They reflect a notion, deep in human consciousness, that eating is never a profane act. Mealtime is sacred time. Every meal is a kind of Seder and Eucharist — a way of being thankful for freedom and food.

These religious meals are also predicated on the presence of family and community. Having Passover and Eucharist alone is almost non-existent. It is as if we were not meant to eat alone. Such programs as Meals on Wheels and eating centers for senior citizens are alternatives to isolation. The average mall guarantees that eating alone need never happen.

Also, we are more inclined to stay related to each other if we eat together. Something happens to us and our conversation when we move from the living room to the dining room. When I say to a guest, "Let's have a drink" or "Please stay for dinner," I have opened up new possibilities for our relationship.

Just as the risen Jesus was known to his disciples around a table ("the breaking of bread"), so we are more fully known and made more vulnerable to one another at a meal. Indeed, mealtime can become a time of intimacy, warmth, and human delight. I'm sure this is why so many deals are struck over lunch and so much reconciliation can take place over dinner. Argument and recrimination seem out of place when people are eating together. Meals are a way of saying, "You are safe with us. You may feel at home, even though you are miles from home."

James Rouse recognized this fact early in his career. He thought shopping and eating could go together naturally and that both could be humanizing experiences. In the late 1960s he introduced what we now see so frequently and what are called by many names — the Food Fair, Food Court, The Eatery, or the Pic-Nic. It is a large circular area with traditional tables at which you can sit or smaller platforms at which you can stand.

As James Rouse said: "We seek a wide variety of eating opportunities in centers, from fine restaurants to fast foods. In two of the most productive centers we have grouped fifteen to twenty over-the-counter eating places around a clean, colorful carnival-like court where men, women, and children can find a wide variety of food, eat quickly, inexpensively, in an attractive environment."[8]

This variety includes the spectrum of ethnic food as well as a broad selection of American food. To add to the uniqueness and to provide for local creativity, few of these fast food restaurants are part of the large national chains: McDonald's, Burger King, Kentucky Fried Chicken, etc.

Malls have continued to provide more space for people to eat. Food has, in fact, become one of the biggest items in most shopping centers and festival marketplaces. A recent trend in a few malls, Beechwood in Cleveland and North Star in San Antonio in particular, is to use the center space of the mall,

SANTA MONICA PLACE
A good example of the eatery: a Food Court with small tables at which you can sit or stand. Courtesy, Rouse Co.

NORTH STAR
The mall "Pic-Nic" is a favorite for families and is invariably intergenerational. These eating areas provide a feeling of "being at home" while you are having fun. Courtesy, Rouse Co.

very close to fountains and trees, as a food court. Eating, then, has become the central activity at the axis mundi, or altar.

One-half of all shoppers will eat something at the mall and thousands of people work within walking distance of most downtown malls. Since they have to eat lunch somewhere, they are more attracted to the festivity and humanness of the center's Pic-Nic. This means lunchtime is one of the busiest times and also the occasion for the most relaxed human inter-action. Cultural historians predict that within a decade only one meal a day will be eaten at home. You can be sure that the mall will use its special appeal to see that the meal retains its celebrative, "holy," and communal nature, and that eating at the mall will be the choice.

Phyllis C. Richman, *Washington Post* restaurant critic summed up the religious significance of food in observing Baltimore's Harbor Place. It "is now the Saturday afternoon outing for kids, the place to stop and eat on the way home from a weekend in New York, the location to meet for a drink after work. It is Baltimore's dinner and lunch and breakfast and late supper and all-day snack shop. It works. And one thing that makes it work is the mix. You can shop for an egg roll, your week's meat order or antique Chinese furniture. You can have a beer or a six-course dinner with Dom Perignon. You can relax indoors or outdoors, in a quiet corner or in the middle of a mob."[9]

Mall as Secular Cathedral

In his recent book, *The Passionate Life*, psychologist and theologian Sam Keen asserts that banks, laboratories, and corporations have taken the place the cathedral once held in our lives. I submit the shopping mall is a more adequate con-temporary analogy to the cathedral. While the mall, to a de-gree, is a child of the banks and corporations (if not of the laboratories), it emerges from a deeper level of our conscious-ness.

Shopping malls and cathedrals serve the same function as banks and corporations in that as Keen says, they "define the nature of reality, provide definition of the good life and status symbols that trigger our desires, and claim to be the center of meaning and value."[10]

In the medieval consensus, the cathedral was a center of felt value. It symbolized the transcendent and, while reflecting many cultural values and limitations, pointed beyond this world to God and heaven where, for the medieval person, true value and treasure lay. The cathedral, therefore, provided a place of orientation, a place where you could get your bearings, and a reminder that life was lived *sub specie aeternitas* (in the light of eternity). The cathedral centered the believer, quasi-believer, and the entire medieval community.

Post–World War II migration from the cities produced the sprawling suburbs and resulted in a great deal of social disorientation. Rouse Company official Scott Ditch says the suburbs have been defined as places where no one knew you before you were thirty years old or after you were sixty-five. The suburbs appealed to the nuclear family and bred the isolation inherent in that peculiarly modern institution. Mom and Dad and the two kids were separated from their grandparents who, along with a lot of older people were poor, disadvantaged, or disabled. In addition, if you were young and single, you did not fit.

The construction of churches was an attempt to orient this homogeneous community. During the 1950s, the church was an effective religious reinforcement of middle-class suburban values and it provided a center for the ex-urban, upwardly mobile, white family. After a generation, it was discovered that church was not relating to all that many people and that it was not a true community center in terms of time and space. It emphasized Sunday activities, and in the case of Protestantism, even retained Sunday morning as the weekly worship time.

Church buildings, if they were open during the week, were

usually off-limits to non-members. And the church's message primarily addressed the "spiritual" part of life, not the total person. This bifurcation of our lives and resultant disorientation were succinctly analyzed in Gibson Winter's book, *The Suburban Captivity of the Church.*

Enter the shopping mall and the whole cultus which surrounds it — a collection of symbols, rituals, and ceremonies attempting to reflect our social self-identity as hardworking, fun-loving conservative folk who are seeking status and trying to better ourselves. That identity also included some anxiety and frustration that the struggle may not realize our intended goals. The mall provided a center, a point of orientation for these suburban ideals and insecurities. It may not have pointed us to "God" or heaven as church does, but it stated that life is more than money, business transactions, and suburban monotony. It was always there, seven days a week, for the whole person.

The mythic imagination and "religious" art found in the malls suggest an experience of otherness, pointing us beyond the rational, the technical, and the utilitarian. The signs are everywhere.

ARCHITECTURE

Specially designed gateways usually mark off entrances to mall parking lots and the territory surrounding the building itself. This informs you immediately that you are going into a distinctive space. It could be a stone or brick entryway decorated by flowers and plants, with the name and logo of the mall prominently displayed.

Having left your car in the parking lot, you probably walk toward the main entrance. There is invariably a primary point of entry, distinguished by an imposing facade, such as at the Galleria in White Plains, New York. The North Star Mall in San Antonio, Texas greets you with a colonnade of Romanesque arches; you walk under a series of stylized Gothic arches as you enter White Marsh Mall near Baltimore; expansive doors and substantial columns grace the front of Smith Haven Mall on Long Island. There may be more modestly decorated entrances, but in each case this "place of passage" or threshold is used to mark off sacred (humanly meaningful) space, whether it be the ordinariness of the outside world from the parking area, or the parking lot from the mall proper. The threshold, while warning of the heterogeneous character of space, allows us to enter another place safely. It reminds us that we are moving from our disordered and familiar world to the ordered and unfamiliar world of the mall.

Because life is created and preserved by the ordering of confusion and by making the stranger feel at home, mall owners and designers go to great lengths to convince us that we are entering not only a comfortable area, but qualitatively different space.

Beyond the entrance, most malls impress us with a sense of height and space which in the cathedral served to express infinity and transcendence. There may be doubt that we experience the same sense of awe as our eyes go skyward in the center of the mall. But we are not unaffected by the sense of spaciousness and height created by the interior design of the mall, and especially by its use of light.

Western designers learned from Roman architecture how helpful light can be in defining interior space. The opening in the dome of the Pantheon gives us the same perception of expansiveness as the skylight in the mall and the clerestory of a cathedral. This sense of expansion provides us with a feeling of freedom and openness, even though we are in the midst of highly organized space.

Although malls will not last as long as cathedrals, there is an attempt by the builders to invest them with durability and permanence. In 1972, for example, Lenox Square Mall placed pertinent contemporary data and memorabilia in a time capsule which was buried in the mall's cornerstone. This capsule is to be reopened in fifty years.

NORTH STAR
A colonnade of Roman arches and fountain greet you at the entrance of this
shopping mall. It bears striking resemblance to a temple. Courtesy, Rouse Co.

GALLERIA MALL, *White Plains, NY*
An imposing, very contemporary design for a gateway.

SMITH HAVEN MALL, *Lake Grove, L.I., New York*
A plain, more traditional entry, but one is nevertheless impressed with its
message of importance. Photo by Mary Zepp

THE SENSUOUS MALL

Having entered the mall, you are bombarded with the reality of this other world. In and through the activity, bustle, and energy, all your senses are affected as they would be in a typical cathedral.

An organ often provided the musical background in the cathedral and was accompanied by conversation, prayer, and singing of the worshipers. The secular modern equivalent of this is music, usually of the Muzak variety, which is piped in the mall. This music is an attempt to smooth the ragged edges of the fretting customer and persuade him or her that here there is a sense of welcome, relief, and comfort. These musical notes have a way of making us more receptive to the message of the mall.

Muzak is notoriously low-brow. It sounds canned, electronic, and sooner or later often produces the opposite effect it intends. Rather than soothing our nerves, it gets on our nerves. To counter this potentially negative result, malls have recently begun playing semi-classical and classical compositions. The Rouse Company has found very positive results from this experiment.

Added to this is the auditory stimulation by the constant din, buzzing, and humming — the sum of all the other sounds being made in the mall.

The aromas of food (meats, fresh baked bread, candies, cookies, fried potatoes, pizzas, etc.), as well as candles, furniture, and cosmetics, combine to keep the olfactory system exercised. These smells are unmistakable proof that you are in a marketplace. The "religious" parallel to this is incense in the cathedral.

The sights are recognizable instantly. Shiny floors, brightly hued banners and colored decorations — not to mention the varied colors in windows and the multiplicity of colors in clothing worn by the crowds — virtually dazzle the observer. In the cathedral, the stained glass, colorful flags, and beautiful statues surrounding the altar are the equivalent.

In addition to the physical closeness between lovers, parents and children, and friends strolling through the mall, there are innumerable opportunities for one to gently feel the textures of clothing fabrics, furniture, and carpets. The same tactile sense is experienced in the cathedral as Catholics dip their hands in holy water, light candles, receive the Eucharist and clasp their hands in prayer while saying the Rosary.

Since most people going to malls find their way to a snack bar, a candy, cookie or ice cream store or, more likely, the food court, our palate is refreshed and our hunger and thirst are assuaged. This is the secular version of the Holy Meal.

Because we do not ordinarily use one sense to the exclusion of another — we do not taste apart from seeing, or feel apart from smelling — the sensual experience of the mall is wholistic. You have the conscious perception of being grasped totally, as a whole, as one is at a well-constructed Catholic worship service.

UNIFORMITY OF MALLS

The mall and cathedral share another similarity. There is a certain uniformity and sameness in each structure. That is not totally true, of course, because there are differences among malls and among cathedrals. There are unique qualities in different cathedrals, from the vaulted Gothic tracery of King's College Chapel at Cambridge, England to the famous steps at Canterbury where Thomas Beckett was murdered to Salisbury with the tallest steeple in England.

In the same way there are idiosyncrasies in malls from the Poinsettia Tree in the Mall in Columbia, Maryland to the Japanese Garden in Fox Hills near Los Angeles to the Clock in Prestonwood Mall in Dallas, Texas.

In the main, however, cathedrals are similar whether you find them in New York, London, or Cologne. Similarly, a mall will provide few surprises for us whether we are in Dallas, Denver, or Chicago. The continuity and similarity, despite geographical differences, enable us to feel at home in the mall. You generally know what you are going to see, whom you will meet, and what behavior you will engage in or observe.

As many clerks and customers reiterate: "It is always the same in the mall." This is one of the mall's appealing characteristics, one of the things that attract us to them. Malls offer us a sense of comfort, security, and reassurance. Notwithstanding a unique characteristic here and there, enough conformity exists among malls to guarantee we will feel at home in them wherever we are.

Significant also is that both the cathedral and the mall can supply a certain anonymity. You are not forced into intimacy or one-on-one relationships. Neither institution is a primary community and for some people this is desirable.

MALL AS SANCTUARY

Long Island's Smith Haven Mall promotes itself like many others when it says it offers a "relaxed, pleasant, non-controversial, family-oriented place, which patrons will view as a sort of refuge from the outside world." Sanctuary, in this context, has come to mean a place where you will not be bothered, harassed, or confronted by something or someone you would find unpleasant. It is where you will feel safe.

It was mentioned earlier that many people find the mall a quiet harbor away from the tensions of life. These people gather at the center to listen to the music and watch the cascading fountains and the carefree antics of children and adults.

People also find relief from the exigencies of the weather. The enclosed climate-controlled mall protects us from the reality and even the knowledge of storms, rain, snow, and wind. Of course, they also preclude our exposure to clouds, sun, moon, leaves turning color, and trees blooming. But for many, this is an acceptable trade-off in return for the former.

The mall is considered crime-free, reinforcing its image as a place of refuge. This perception is grounded in a good deal of evidence. While some burglaries (mostly car break-ins) and assaults have been reported in mall parking lots, such occurrences rarely happen within the mall itself. Customers are not nearly as apt to be mugged, nor are shopkeepers as likely to be robbed or vandalized in the mall as they are on a city street or in their home. You will not meet panhandlers in the mall; indeed, most malls limit the possibility of your being solicited by anyone, from Hare Krishna devotees to the Girl Scouts. Mall patrons are usually only stopped by people conducting marketing research.

Security officers are always present, in and out of uniform. They are usually well trained. The Rouse Company is particularly concerned that their officers know how to treat disorderly teenagers. Frank Riedy, head of security in Columbia Mall, says, "We see ourselves as public relation persons for the Rouse Company. We do not counsel in any direct sense, but if we see someone being disruptive in the mall, we will say to the person or persons in a diplomatic way: 'This behavior may be dangerous to others and we want to put the welfare of the mall first. We would like your cooperation. And if you persist, we will have to resort to sterner measures. But we ask you to be ladies and gentlemen.'" Security personnel often have to serve as a "cop" and a "counselor." And, generally, they succeed.

The fortress image, often associated with the malls and just as often down-played by public relations people, remains a serious criticism. But problems associated with this image are outweighed by the safety people feel and expect to find at the mall.

MALL AS "PATRON" OF THE ARTS

The Catholic Church, with its sense of universality (catholicity), would always welcome the creative work of people while celebrating the work of God. The creativity of the human spirit did not seem out of place displayed prominently in the cathedral. It was never a substitute for the altar, but could be found very close to it.

The Easter Vigil illustrates the capacity of Catholicism to embrace, if not baptize, all of life. At some vigils, symbols of community organizations are brought into church and exhibited on walls and doors. At the appropriate moment, a priest will sprinkle holy water on the insignia, symbol, emblem, flag or banner of these community organizations as a sign that the entire community is again being blessed and renewed.

By displaying the work of human hands, the cathedral gives dignity to community labor, bestows value on everyday life, and gives meaning to the sincere efforts of the humblest person. It can link our life and livelihood to divine significance and meaning. We see ourselves as part of the wider picture, as fitting into God's plan. Paul Tillich called this the "structural unity of our infinite manifoldness."[11]

The cathedral's ability to assimilate disparate secular symbols and enterprises, as well as to give them a certain sanction, is an attempt to simplify. It makes more coherent relationships that may be considered complicated and tension-producing in the outside world.

Formal rituals like the Easter Vigil are, of course, not found in the malls. But the way in which the mall attempts to represent community life is not dissimilar to the cathedral's attempt to reflect the significant human dimensions of the neighboring community. You can find an interesting assortment of responses to the fine arts, for example, primarily sculpture and painting in malls.

The cathedral after all was a patron of the arts — in painting, sculpture, architecture, music, and drama. The mall itself is a form of art which includes music, drama, and literature. Malls will not soon compete seriously with cathedrals in this regard, but they do have their own murals, sculpture, or other unique art work. The massive eagle in Crossroads Mall in Boulder, Colorado and the large modern sculpture by Alexander Calder in Smith Haven Mall on Long Island are classic examples. These are obviously not prefabricated by a corporate chain store.

In fact, the malls, surprisingly enough, have an abundance of contemporary, abstract, and even avant-garde art forms, especially in sculpture. These pieces would be more at home in a modern art museum than in a conservative business establishment, much less in our hometown or village square. Somehow, the mall can absorb all this. In what is otherwise a middle-class institution, the mall becomes one vast art gallery in its walkways and corridors. The artists are often present, willing to talk with you, and eager to sell you their work.

Permanent art displays and periodic art shows are matters of considerable pride and prestige for some malls, enhancing their image as showplaces. William R. Anderson and Herbert Sprouse, writing in *Museum News* (October 1984) recall Victor Gruen's ideal of the shopping mall as a center that would "integrate community services, social and cultural activities, and shopping—that would, in other words, create urbanity in suburbia." In the article, "Museums in the Marketplace," they indicate how many new museums have made shopping malls their permanent home. They cite Bellevue Art Museum in Bellevue Square, Bellevue, Washington, the Los Angeles Children's Museum in the Los Angeles Mall, Los Angeles, California, and the Museum of Scientific Discovery at Strawberry Square, Harrisburg, Pennsylvania.

In 1977, the Rouse Company established its Art in the Marketplace Program and according to Anderson and Sprouse, perhaps the most famous branch museum in a shopping center was the Boston Museum of Fine Arts two-year experiment with a 12,000 square foot gallery above two floors of shops in Faneuil Hall Marketplace in Boston.

Two other significant temporary exhibits in the past decade were provided by The Franklin Institute Science Museum in Philadelphia's Gallery Mall at Market East (for five years) and the Boston Museum of Fine Arts two-year exhibit in Faneuil Hall Marketplace. The malls appear to be saying that "if the masses do not go to art museums, then we will bring the museum to the masses." Perhaps, in this sense, the mall can be said to be a patron of the arts.

MALL AS TOURIST ATTRACTION

Malls are certainly "more than" a marketplace for the American Association of Retired Persons. The organization publishes an annual "Mall Festival Series." According to an AARP News Bulletin (December 1983), the "four-day festivals of major retail shopping complexes throughout the nation combine informational displays on Association programs/services aimed at enhancing the lifestyle of older adults, accompanied by merchandising displays from the private sector." Companies such as Prudential Insurance, Campbell Soup, Kellogg, and General Motors will sponsor exhibits and display one or more of their products.

The Association-sponsored series of twenty shopping mall festivals include Altamonte Mall in Altamonte Springs, Florida, Winrock Mall in Albuquerque, New Mexico, and Westminster Mall near Westminster, California. When a mall decides to sponsor a special event appropriate for older consumers, it will inform the AARP and that mall will be placed on the series schedule.

The AARP connection is representative of just how much the mall has become a tourist attraction. This is particularly true of the festival marketplaces designed by James Rouse. Harborplace has become a strong magnet attracting tourists to Baltimore. "If you come to Baltimore, you simply must see Harborplace," boasts the city tourist bureau, as well as many proud citizens of Baltimore. The same is true of Lenox Square, which according to its estimates, attracts 30 to 40 percent of Atlanta's three million annual tourists.

Many mall public relations offices say one reason the day

after a major holiday is often one of the busiest of the year is that families take their out-of-town relatives to nearby malls. These tourists swell the large crowds naturally expected after a holiday like Thanksgiving. But malls are also crowded the day after Christmas, Easter, and other holidays.

Undoubtedly such festival marketplaces now draw more sightseers than large urban cathedrals. Travel agencies often include visits to cathedrals on their European tours. There is every indication that malls will soon be the American counterpart for metropolitan tourist bureaus.

• 5 •

Concluding Observations: From Lenox Square to Bel Air

An Attempt to Retain the Personal

Saturday night in Bel Air was not just a temporal or geographical reference. It was a metaphor for a personal community exchanging goods and services, and, at the same time, having fun. Lenox Square represents the average EMAC trying hard to be the sort of primary community that Bel Air was. Both Saturday night in Bel Air and Lenox Square illustrate the supra-commercial nature of shopping—the "more than" of the marketplace.

For two decades now James Rouse and other imaginative mall developers have tried to recapture the town square and the small American village in their large regional shopping malls. And, as I have attempted to show, the EMAC is successful to a considerable degree.

The EMAC tried to recreate the marketplace as more than a place for business; it was also to be a meeting place, a space set apart for a community involved in varying degrees of ceremony and ritual. With the addition of natural setting elements (light, water, and trees), the mall meets the needs of many urban and suburban folks. These huge shopping centers, each new one dwarfing its predecessors, try to neutralize the polarization Paul Wheatley suggested would likely occur when a community shifts from *Gemeinschaft* to *Gesellschaft* (from personal to impersonal community). He said there is a tendency to move from an emphasis on status to an emphasis on contract, from primary relationships to secondary ones, from *societas* to *civitas*, from living to contrived, from organic to plastic.

The shopping mall, in attempting to resist this trend, no doubt falls somewhere between the poles. It never completely reproduces the primary nature of human relationships, the face-to-face, first-name basis of Saturday night in Bel Air. Lenox Square could hardly be expected to pull that off. On the other hand, the mall never finally surrenders to the depersonalization, anonymity, and coldly contractual character of most urban life.

Still, the mall is relatively successful in retaining the "high touch" of shopping as experienced in Bel Air. Customers can interact with clerks behind counters, rather than trying to catch up with them as they wander down aisles in self-service discount stores, supermarkets, and department stores.

The EMAC endeavored to reclaim the personal by its emphasis on centers, its attention to detail, its cleanliness, its desire to have shops look "natural," its expectation that shopping would be festive and gay. This is not to mention the possibility of regularly scheduled art shows and musical concerts, community outreach programs, and the ceremonial activities which occur at the center. In short, the mall tries to be sensitive to the needs—cultural, social, and religious—of the whole person.

The malls' religious symbolism and the ritual life found in them imply that for many people they are "real" places—places where there is a certain sense of reality about the sacred and the humanly meaningful experiences found there.

In 1983, James Rouse commented on the favorable response

to the large shopping center and to the more recent festival marketplace. He attributed their success in part to society's reaction to the "fractured living" of suburban subdivisions. It is also a reaction he said, "to the high-tech computerized, televised, cellophane-wrapped chain store society which has emerged in recent years — a reaction which has generated a yearning for the warm, the intimate, and the personal relationships with merchants — owners behind the counter — a yearning for the color, fragrance, texture, and variety of the true marketplace."[1]

This reference contains a veiled criticism of the large regional malls which encircle our cities. Despite its best efforts to recall the village square, the EMAC all too often is perceived as sterile, antiseptic, and "cellophane-wrapped." The atmosphere is not sufficiently warm, intimate, and personal.

The "yearning" for these qualities is more fully satisfied — or so it is hoped — by the festival marketplace, which is now an identifiable shopping area and not just the ambience of a large mall. The festival marketplace is presently understood to be a smaller, more emotionally and physically manageable space than the acres of shops anchored by four or five department stores. People have an ontological vocation — that is, their very being calls out for the personal, for experiences on a more human scale.

What are the shortcomings of the large EMAC — the shortcomings which, in some cases, forced the creation of a smaller, more organic shopping center? Why do we keep wanting to find Bel Air in Lenox Square? Why do we keep looking for that corner drugstore to hang out in? From a religious studies point of view we ask: As human centers, what are the profane and "unreal" dimensions of malls?

First, many people are put off by the obviously synthetic character of the malls. The creative chaos of the village, the inherent tension in a dynamic community, are minimized in the EMAC. The EMAC, unlike Bel Air, does not recognize the brokenness of human or natural life and its value in the total human picture. The orderliness of the mall is sometimes uncanny and oppressive.

There is no soliciting, leafleting, or begging by religious and political devotees or the poor. The fabricated streets have no telephone poles or fire hydrants. You long for grass between bricks and sidewalks made uneven by tree roots.

Mall developers and managers brag about having everything under one roof. But Patrick Butler, writing in *Saturday Review* over a decade ago, anticipated this inherent weakness of the average EMAC.

> What I really want is to get out from under that one roof. I'd like to walk down a real sidewalk with cracks in it, feel some real weather in my face, and maybe just cut over there across the street to the pawnbroker next to that bar and study the ukeleles in the window.[2]

And John Zeisel, a sociologist of environmental behavior, is critical of the claim that the mall has something for everyone. After awhile you get bored. "That's because although there's something for everyone, there's not a lot for any one person. You go (to Faneuil Hall) for the experience, like a scenic vista. Like scenery you remember it, but you don't watch it for long."

In addition, these malls don't offer the homespun characters who made Bel Air so fascinating. You find identifiable groups in the mall — the teens, the elderly, and middle-aged matrons — but not the unique individuals.

Secondly, malls appeal, generally, to the middle class and, sometimes as I have mentioned, to the upper class. All the advantages plugged by the mall public relations office — safety, cleanliness, comfort, fun, relaxation — cost money. The shopkeepers' rent and overhead, much more than that paid by comparable store owners in a strip center, on a main street, or downtown, is naturally passed on to the consumer in higher retail prices.

While the middle class is willing to accept the higher prices as a trade-off for these advantages, a lot of people simply don't have that kind of money. The mall is predicated upon a certain elitism, affluence, luxury, and the availability of spare time. I have heard older persons and the poor say, "I don't have any fun shopping."

Shopping can hardly be a festive affair for those who must manage their low or fixed income in such a way that they have just enough for the necessities of life. The "more than" of the marketplace is beyond their means and is the source of a good deal of derision and resentment. The extravagance of the average mall as compared to a store in a rural or urban slum brings into bold relief the disparity between the haves and have-nots.

Furthermore, since malls are basically white institutions, blacks and other minorities do not usually feel at home in them. Robert Campbell, a practicing architect in Cambridge, Massachusetts and a mall critic, notes the "social homogeneity" of such malls as Faneuil Hall. "Black people do come, but they are not common. As a group, blacks don't feel welcome." He hastens to add that this is not an "architectural nor a management problem, but rather a problem in the nature of Boston."

A few malls, such as Mondawmin Mall in Baltimore, have a predominantly black clientele, but this is unusual. Malls, like churches and schools, follow and reflect housing patterns. These residential zones presuppose a certain economic status which precludes many minority persons.

Actually, there were few blacks in the park in Bel Air on Saturday night, although the black neighborhood was just a block away from Main Street. Their invisibility on that night and in the contemporary malls is as much a statement about our society's racism as it is about the "park" in Bel Air and festival marketplaces.

Thirdly, the safety issue in malls has to be reexamined continually. On the whole, the public perception of the safety of the EMAC is relatively close to the reality. This is true in spite of the highly acclaimed TV docudrama *Adam*, where a little boy vanished from a mall after his mother left him alone for a few minutes.

I have talked with security officers around the country who say the biggest problems faced are theft (shoplifting) and an occasional mugging. "You can tell who the suburban women are," they say, "by how they hold their pocketbooks. Women from the city clutch them while suburban women swing theirs."

These security personnel add that if any serious crime takes place, it is usually in the parking lot. Security is not only being increased in some malls during the holiday season, but there are additional security people roaming the parking lots.

Besides petty theft, the other main concern of security officers is finding lost children. "Mothers are sometimes too careless about their children — walking ahead of them, for instance. Then they expect us to find the children for them," said one security person in Philadelphia.

The mall, trying to be the small community and to allay the fear and anxiety associated with big city life, counts on security personnel to provide a perception of safety. Although there are exceptions, the public is generally not disappointed.

And finally, the expansion of these large regional shopping complexes often means unfortunately that the malling of America becomes the mauling of communities. Environmentalists have worried about the disturbance of rural areas, the disorientation of small communities, and the exploiting of prime farmland.

The increase in traffic, the over-taxing of sewage treatment plants, the expansion of population, the widening of roads and the creation of new ones, naturally have local residents concerned. Ironically, the creation of a natural environment in the mall is often accompanied by the destruction of the natural environment outside the mall.

Recognizing these shortcomings, and in spite of the outright cynicism of some critics, the average shopper prefers the EMAC to the traditional downtown shopping area or the small town, with its attendant parking problem, limited selection of goods, and possibilities for carnival. The EMAC is still being built in significant numbers and people continue to flock to them.

The new EMAC, however, will be smaller, although it will also significantly enough, continue to be "more than" a marketplace. This is in response to the need of a sizable section of our population for more safe, intimate, and human places. Notice how many malls bring in farmer's wagons to sell fresh fruits and vegetables, or add kiosks and pushcarts to give the effect of miniature stores. The point is that the perception of smallness must be maintained even in a large space.

The future of retailing probably lies with the EMAC, on the one hand, continuing to strive to be personal and, on the other hand, the festival marketplace, which is physically smaller, attempting to ensure more personal accessibility.

An advantage of these newer festival marketplaces is that they are usually built at or near former commercial centers: shorelines, harbors, waterfronts, or old downtown business districts. Continuity with the traditions of the site and familial memories usually combine to create a flourishing market.

Old Mistick Village in New London, CT, was a forerunner of this smaller center. On the west coast near Los Angeles is Fisherman's Village in Marina del Rey. Both of these shopping centers are attempts to reproduce 18th-century New England villages and both arouse deliberately our nostalgia.

For the past five years, the Rouse Company and the Enterprise Development Corporation have concentrated on the return to the personal and the intimate in their design and construction of shopping centers, without eliminating the festive atmosphere they still insist is necessary for a marketplace.

While these smaller marketplaces usually have centers,

they often do not have an elaborate center court or symmetrical quadrants, anchored by large department stores, leading to a ceremonial center. But, as in the large mall, personal interaction is encouraged and there is a rich ceremonial life. The monthly, yearly and other seasonal rituals, usually performed in the EMAC, are seen on a smaller scale out-of-doors adjacent to the "village" stores. Baltimore's Harborplace and Boston's Faneuil Hall have excellent facilities for these events. The "more than" of the marketplace remains intact.

So it seems that the EMAC and the more recent festival marketplace are trying continually to emulate Bel Air — the small, primary, face-to-face community. Something human demands it. We like to see the butcher carving meat before our eyes, that baker bringing bread from the oven to the counter; we want to see and relate to people, not mannequins. We want prefabrication held to a minimum. We desire places to visit, to bring our friends to socialize and "see the sights" just as was once done Saturday night in Bel Air.

Malls are contemporary versions of that age-old combination of commerce and community. They will continue to fill the void created by our social institutions' failure in providing centers of ritual and meaning.

Some of us are interested in religious studies because we are interested in people. People do religious things; they symbolize and ritualize their lives and desire to be in a community. What piqued my interest in shopping malls initially was their concrete expressions of all three of these religious impulses. Quadrilateral architecture, calendrical rituals, replications of natural settings, and attempts to be people places and objects of pilgrimage, all illustrate homo religiosus. The shopping mall as a ceremonial center, the shopping mall as "more than" a marketplace, is one way contemporary people are meeting their needs for renewal and reconnection, essential ingredients of religious and human life.

· 6 ·

The Mall Is Not Over

Architecture — particularly explicitly sacred architectures like temples, tombs, pyramids, palaces, mosques, and monasteries — constitute inexhaustible funds of otherness. Religious buildings arise as human creations, but they persist as transforming, life-altering environments; they are at once expressions and sources of religious experiences. As created and creator, a religious building manifests human aspirations and intentions: the meaning of such buildings, however, "not occasionally, but always" surpasses its original intention. Once erected, architects immediately lose control of the significance and meaning of their projects. What the builders have in mind is, invariably, but the first in an endless stream of ideas and sensations that their architectonic creations will evoke. Consequently, as *homo religiosus* live and worship in, reflect upon, and "play with" the built structure in their environment, they endlessly disrupt old meanings —, and awaken fresh ones. (Lindsay Jones, *Twin City Tales: A Hermeneutical Reassessment of Tula and Chichén Itzá*)

The central force used to be the schools or the church. That is not the case anymore. A mall, if properly managed and structured in terms of its services, can meet those needs from another perspective. (Janice A. Davis, a businesswoman and member of the Silver Spring, Maryland, task force, which is considering building a mega-mall in her community)

Heinrich Hermann, a Harvard graduate student of the history and theory of architecture with an academic interest in comparative religion, is writing a doctoral dissertation on the spiritual aspects of physical environment. In it he says that architecture can "make visible the intersection between human life in the finite material world and the seeming infinity of space and time." Some environments, says Craig Lambert, author of "Space and Spirit," evoke a temporary escape or sanctuary from a fast pace of life. He writes: "Spaces that embody a spiritual dimension make us feel protected and cared for, and allow us the freedom to rest, to endure, to be rejuvenated. Such spaces can interrupt the flow of daily life and lift us onto a different place. Making us pause, they reorient us and induce us to become detached observers of reality — to reflect on what lies hidden beneath its outer appearance."[1]

This description certainly applies to those for whom the mall is more than a marketplace, which is the thesis of this book. I would, however, substitute the word "sacred," as it was discussed at length in Chapters 1 and 3, for Lambert's use of "spiritual."

As far back as 1985, William Kowinski, an authority on malls, noted that it is the mall as a

> large and controlled environment, filled with amenities but directed toward a single purpose, that links it thematically with other dominating environments of our time — condominium buildings and villages, planned communities, convention centers, domed stadiums, airports, office and high-tech manufacturing campuses, megastructure hotels and all their combinations. They are often physically as well as stylistically linked, creating a kind of mall-condo continuum across the urban and suburban landscape of America.[2]

This observation reflects the proliferation in the past decade of mall-like complexes and explains why I discuss ballparks and airports at some length in this chapter.

I learned the phenomenological method from reading Mircea Eliade and listening to the lectures of Will Herberg, two more disparate intellectuals you could not find. Herberg particularly stressed the descriptive nature of this method, in which judgment is suspended and value is bracketed out. Eliade emphasized the analytical aspect of phenomenology, that is, the attempt to find patterns and meanings and to seek the religious intention of what was being described. A final piece of phenomenology is that the observer sees *as* the other sees, not just *with* the other. It is this empathic mode that underscores Rabbi Jacob Neusner's observation that "the more I get to know you, the more of myself I see in you and the less strange you become to me. And the more I get to know you, the more of you I see in myself and the stranger I become to myself."

I am aware of some of the criticisms of Eliade and the attempted deconstruction of his place in the study of the history of religions, led in large measure by Jonathan Z. Smith.[3] Smith and others say that there are more pattern and not enough content, more universality and not enough historicity, and more complexity in *homo religiosus* than Eliade's reductionism implies. Another critic, Matei Calinescu, says that Eliade's hermeneutic is too imaginative and finds meaning where there is none.[4]

I acknowledge the flaws in Eliade's project, the danger of imposing meaning on phenomena rather than extracting meaning from them. Nevertheless, I ventured on with the hope that my presuppositions would remain as much out of the way as possible, that I would elicit rather than impose, that I would be self-critical enough to refer to what happens at the mall and not what happens in my mind. I wanted to be an exegete, not an eisegete.

To enter into the Eliade/Smith et al. debate, however, is not the purpose of this book. It is to say that my own reading of Eliade finds him sufficiently appreciative of history *and* cultural content to be a helpful hermeneut for my attempt to understand shopping malls. I was guided, more than I realized, by the next to last sentence in David Cave's book *Mircea Eliade's Vision for a New Humanism,* where in virtual Eliadian language he says, "Every place, every experience, every moment of time is potentially rich in meaning if we are willing to ask the hermeneutical question. 'What does it mean?' "[5] The trick is to find that meaning as honestly and carefully as possible.

The Call of the Mall

Two thousand years after Trajan's three-storied mall in Rome (c. 112 C.E.), with its 100 clothing, vegetable, and tool shops and its great hall for customers to socialize; four decades after Southdale, the first EMAC, was built in 1956 in Edina, Minnesota; and ten years after the mother of malls (West Edmonton in Alberta) was completed in 1986, urban/suburban malls continue to bring vast numbers of people together in a communal event ostensibly to purchase but also to be relieved of what, a generation ago, David Reisman called "the lonely crowd," our unspoken feelings of personal isolation and failing individualism.[6] The mall continues to affect the way we meet each other, exercise, play, invest our money, even care for our health and medical needs. Mating rituals, the pursuit of happiness, and education are found at these new and truly "general" stores. We now give directions with reference to malls. "You know where the mall is? Well, go about a mile and a half, turn left, and you are on the street where we live."

The "more than" that I discussed at some length over ten years ago in Chapter 1 has been repeated again and again by mall watchers and culture commentators. Nothing supports my original thesis more than this striking excerpt from Susan Reimer's column in the August 6, 1995, edition of the *Baltimore Sun:*

> To squash our uncertainty, malls are now built to distract us. They have evolved from climate-controlled, one-stop shopping in a place free from noise and traffic. They are now sophisticated architectural masterpieces. Galleries, the perfect word.
>
> Multilevel atriums and curved escalators, rich woods, polished brass, marble floors, exotic flora and gurgling fountains, the mingled aromas of international foods. Huge, suspended sculptures and soothing music. A rush of sensations to beat boredom and loneliness and routine.
>
> Researchers tell retailers that the consumer wants not just hot pretzels and Teva sandals, but also an *experience*. Malls sell not just goods, but good times. And they are safe good times.

> After work and home, Americans spend the most time at the Mall. According to time-use studies, it is part of our week, our routine, our lifestyle. "The Mall has become a pleasure zone," said Mindy Roches, of Towson. "Almost like an erogenous zone."

I am writing this in November, but I notice that the local mall has already programmed its Christmas holiday Muzak and announced that Santa will arrive before Thanksgiving in time for a photo shoot with children on his knee. In fact, the annual retail binge, accompanied by festivity, entertainment, and personal services, is in full swing. Malls were meant for the Christmas season — the quintessential shopping spree and the optimum time for social bonding. If you hear a giant sucking sound, it is this festive commercial vortex magnetically drawing folks to the center — a lemminglike stampede reflecting mall mania.

The International Council of Shopping Centers, the trade organization that provides reliable information about the ups and downs of consumer trends, has ample statistical evidence that malls continue to be a part of daily life. Most shoppers have at least four malls they visit beyond their favorite one. Seven out of ten U.S. adults shop in malls each week, exceeding the number of Americans who go to church. The omnipresence of malls in our lives, physically if not psychically, is seen in a remark made a few years ago by Russell Baker: "Either America is a shopping center, or the one shopping center in existence is moving around the country with the speed of light."

We are more malled than ever. Malls have become regular themes for columnists. For example, they have been the subject of at least three of Erma Bombeck's columns in 1994–1995. "Malling has become a verb in this country. To many women, a day without a visit to the mall is like a day without sunshine," writes Erma.[7] A further illustration of the omnipresence of malls is Milton Bradley's Electronic Mall Madness: The Talking Shopping Spree Game, released in 1989 for ages nine and up.

Films are now routinely including malls as part of their plots or scenery. In addition to the critical statement made by *Dawn of the Dead,* others, such as *Back to the Future, Logan's Run, Commando, Running Man, Mall Rats, Scenes from a Mall,* and *The Mighty Ducks,* reflect the fact that malls are naturally a meeting place for us.

Furthermore, witness how the use of "mall" has entered our discourse. There is a long list of phrases now found in our language, both spoken and written, that indicate the linguistic influence of the mall.

mall mania	mall nutrition
mall talk	malled out
mall around	mall rat
mall or nothing	mallaise
a mall world after all	mallhead
mall-o-ween	mal de mall
getting malled	mall-lingering
mall hopping	mall-adjusted
malleable	malladies
It's mall in a day's work.	Deck the malls.

I've heard of a group of folks who have weekly evening meetings in a mall and refer to themselves as "A mall and the night visitors." Bumper stickers have appeared to reflect this mania and perhaps to promote it: "Buy until you die," "Shop until you drop," "Shut up and shop," and a new Cartesian reductionism! — "I consume; therefore I am."

While the rate of increase in the construction of large regional malls (over 400,000 square feet) has slowed, in the past decade malls, in order to compete with a slightly increasing number of the old strip shopping centers, have stressed two new sets of activities beyond retailing. These newly emphasized trends are service and entertainment.

There is a stark increase in the number and variety of *non-commercial* services. What used to take us to many different offices and what used to take up a good deal of time and travel now can be accomplished in one stop at the mall. A short list will suffice to illustrate the multiplicity of options:

express mail drop	optometry
ATMs	counseling center
fax machines	mammogram
auto service	child care
dentist	worship, in some cases
mani/pedicure	
local, state, and federal government branch offices	

More and more, the mall is curved to fit the wrist: it aims to please, to fulfill, to be all things to all people. The mall itself, not a particular shop or store, has become the destination. The apparent assumption is that you can find anything you want at the mall. As they say, "It's all in the mall." We have here one-stop shopping raised to infinity. All of this, mind you, is in addition to purchasing the usual retail items or, for many, *instead* of buying them.[8]

By far, the newest aspect of mall development, especially in the large regional ones, is the entertainment centers. They have become virtually the center ring in such malls as Canada's West Edmonton and the Mall of America. (But more about this later.) It is little wonder, then, that Saul Katz, a vice-president for Triple Five Corporation, owned and operated by the Ghermezian brothers, who built West Edmonton, said, "This mall is a form of urban infrastructure catering to people's lifestyle requirement and serving their social, psychological needs, as well as their material ones."[9]

It is axiomatic that malls have become the new downtown, main street, or village square. The returns are not in, however, as to whether or to what extent the mall is effectively serving us in the same organic way. The checkerboard atop the cracker barrel seems destined for the dustbins of Sturbridge Village or other quaint replications of the 19th-century general store.

With the arrival of the EMAC, we have crossed the Rubicon of shopping. Once people have visited these consumer wonderlands, they probably won't want to go back to the village store. The historical and cultural context that produced the mall will not soon disappear.

The cybermall, or shopping via the Internet, is the new competitive context on the horizon, however. This kind of shopping is the most immediate threat to our weekly treks to the mall. Jeanne Marie Lukas, in an article entitled "Of Mice and Malls," said in effect, "Everything you need is on that disk at the click of the mouse."[10] For the committed cybershopper, that mouse will eventually allow you to stroll through and windowshop at the 370 malls found in "The Shopper" in your Internet directory.

And what is better, you can enter the shops and engage in the virtual reality of interactive consumption. I am told you can program your computer screen with your measurements, design a suit or dress, try it on, see how it looks, and then decide to purchase it or not. Cyberspecialists say that by 2010, 55 percent of the nation's shopping will be done without benefit of the usual storelike space.

Another competitor to the malls that has developed in the past decade is the rapid growth of so-called power centers, the "big box" retailers or, as they are sometimes called, the "killer stores." The latter are huge discount warehouses with sky-high shelves, such as Price Club, Target, Sam's Club, and, to a lesser degree, Wal-Mart, Lowe's, and Home Depot.

These stores are not just for the average Joe (the vast majority of the shoppers here are men) or weekend warriors who must do-it-themselves. Former president Bush, former vice-president Quayle, and a number of Hollywood celebrities have been sighted there. One goes here not to socialize but to buy. The appeal is a lesser amount of money spent in a limited amount of time with a Zenlike concentration on the business at hand. There is no fun here and no specially programmed Muzak. All space is used for merchandise, with the exception of the necessary room for offices.

Observers have called this power-center shopping a return to "hunting and gathering" or to "treasure hunting," if not to scavenging and foraging. Certainly, there are quests and conquests here. One is reminded of the cargo cults formed by South Pacific communities after contact with the postindustrialized West and Japan. Marc Fisher quotes David Givens, a research anthropologist: "[The Price Club] doesn't just sell products; it sells trophies. When you come home with a huge supply of toilet paper, and the man enters the house with this, he is truly the conquering hero."[11]

It is problematic whether the average America suburb can support the retail critical mass provided by these mammoth commercial hubs. There are pendulum swings in retailing as in all historical reality. One thing is relatively certain: malls, with their combination of convenience, service, entertainment, *and* retailing, will continue into the foreseeable future.

The Megamalls

WEST EDMONTON MALL, ALBERTA, CANADA

What follows are not references to the Taj Mahal or the Sistine Chapel:

> "I was stunned. It absolutely made my mouth drop. It was unbelievable. The most amazing place I've ever seen and I've been around. . . ."
> Floating like a giant white whale on the snowy prairies of Canada is the West Edmonton Mall, the Moby Dick of shopping centers. The family of Middle Eastern rug merchants who built it call it "the eighth wonder of the world."[12]

Language is exhausted as people attempt to describe this Valhalla for shoppers, this end-of-the-rainbow malldom. "Beyond compare. Incredible. Unbelievable. A bedazzling jewel. A fascinating combination of fashion, fun, and fantasy." So goes the advertising brochure for the West Edmonton Mall. William Kowinski quotes *Toronto Globe* reporter Ian Brown as saying,

"[It's] like turning on all the channels of the TV at the same time."[13] Here are mystery, enchantment, mesmerism — all that we in religious studies say constitutes religious awe in the presence of spatial otherness and grandeur.

What is being described is the world's biggest mall, located in Alberta, Canada. It has, of course, found its niche in the *Guinness Book of World Records*. West Edmonton was built by Jacob Ghermezian and Sons — Nader, Bahman, Eskandar, Raphael — natives of Iran. They came to Montreal in 1959, having made a fortune selling carpets. In 1967 they moved to Edmonton, attracted by prospects in the oil business. They soon formed the Triple Five Corporation and became real estate developers, of which West Edmonton, constructed in 1986, is their crowning glory.

The gargantuan nature of this mall, its sheer monumentality, is incomparable. Here is a sample of the mosts, the greatests, and the highests:

> 3.8 million square feet of retail area
>
> 800 stores
>
> 58 entrances
>
> parking lot for 20,000 cars
>
> area of 110 acres (roughly 108 football fields)
>
> a full-scale replica of Columbus' 80-foot-long flagship, the *Santa Maria*
>
> a 2-block replica of Bourbon Street
>
> a 700-person nightclub
>
> a zoo
>
> a church (Marketplace Chapel)
>
> an 18-hole miniature golf course
>
> an ice rink (home of the Edmonton Oilers)

Topping off this extravaganza is the 5-acre water park called Fantasyland, the world's largest indoor amusement park, complete with its own beach and waves. West Edmonton also boasts one of the world's highest steel roller coasters, with cars going more than 60 miles an hour. The mall's aisles and corridors are decorated with millions of dollars in bronze statues and sculptures. This is not to mention the 138 places to eat, from lowbrow fast food, to middle-brow gourmet, to highbrow elegant.

After visiting West Edmonton, a delegation from China, led by Vice-Premier Yao Yilin, was determined to duplicate the project in China. According to *Chicago Tribune* writer Jon Anderson, an Edmonton wit quickly helped them with a name, "The Great Mall of China." William Kowinski is surely correct when he says, "For all its size and strangeness, West Edmonton Mall is less an exception than a summing up of what the shopping mall is all about."[14] There is not a difference in kind, only in degree, from Lenox Square in Atlanta to West Edmonton in Alberta.

MALL OF AMERICA, BLOOMINGTON, MINNESOTA

Five minutes from Minneapolis-St. Paul International Airport and ten minutes from downtown is the wonderland of American retailing. America's largest mall was built in 1992, but as the mall advertisement states, "Anyone who thinks that the Mall of America is just a big mall probably also thinks that the Grand Canyon is just a big hole in the ground."

Superlatives abound to outline its size. It is larger in square footage than Red Square and could hold twenty Saint Peter's Basilicas. This crème de la crème of American malls has space enough to contain seven Yankee Stadiums or all the gardens of Buckingham Palace and is constructed with twice as much steel as the Eiffel Tower. It holds the biggest indoor planting of trees and shrubs, with climate-controlled facilities, and the world's largest twin parking garage (13,000 cars).

There are nearly four hundred shops laid out along 13 miles of corridors (sidewalks?) and anchored by old reliables — Bloomingdale's, Macy's, Nordstrom's, and Sears. The Mall of America has its own zip code, school, boxing ring, and archery range. Within the mall is Knott's Camp Snoopy, a 76-acre park that is the largest indoor theme entertainment park in America. Created and operated by Knott's Berry Farm of southern California, it is the mall's feature attraction, where visitors have not lost their capacity to be awed, shocked, or overwhelmed. You can "pan for real gold in an authentic mining sluice and take home your claim."

The mall itself reflects a quadrilateral division. Its four sections are East Broadway, West Market, North Garden, and South Avenue. The Mall of America is located on the former site of Metropolitan Stadium, home of the Minnesota Twins and Vikings. In the northwest corner of Camp Snoopy, embedded in a faux stone floor, is a five-sided plaque resembling home plate. Exactly 520 feet away, in the southeast corner of the amusement park, affixed to a wall above the floor is a fold-down seat, the approximate spot where, on June 3, 1967, Harmon Killebrew hit the longest home run in the Twins' history. It has become the holy of holies in a sacred center. Some doubted whether this mall would be a success. It has become one of the major tourist attractions in America, with one hundred thousand visitors a day.

THE AMERICAN DREAM MALL, SILVER SPRING, MARYLAND

In 1994 an advisory group, eleven residents and eight county officials, from Silver Spring, a suburban Maryland community just outside the nation's capital, made a trip to Edmonton and Minneapolis to explore their malls. A mall was being planned for the Silver Triangle, which borders the District of Columbia and the two suburban counties of Montgomery and Prince George's.

It will consist of 2 million square feet (the Pentagon is 3.7 million square feet) on a 27-acre complex, cost over $500 million, and be developed by none other than the dream team of Ghermezian brothers who built West Edmonton and Mall of America.

This retail and entertainment complex is designed to include a 500-room fantasy theme hotel and an amusement park (Galaxyland) with an accompanying wave pool for 3,000 swimmers (Hawaii has come to us!). Time would fail to tell of its planned 1,100-seat ice rink, indoor roller coaster, and underground parking garages for 2,000 cars.

This is a work in progress, however. From August to November 1995 the Silver Spring Advisory Committee responded to county pressure and scaled down some of the original size. There is a felt need to make the proposed mall more community oriented, rather than a templated West Edmonton or Mall of America. Said one committee member, "We want elements of a town center which interact with the surrounding urban landscape. This is a more positive step."[15] That landscape includes one of the wealthiest African-American populations in the United States and the cultural diversity next door in the nation's capital.

One thing is certain: it will not be the massive enterprise once envisioned. The community group wants less footage for the amusement park and fewer hotel rooms. It wants more open space, a real need of the urban area in which the mall is planned. There is a possibility, however, for the mall to form a partnership with nearby Takoma Park Campus of Montgomery College to encourage, perhaps underwrite, a program of entrepreneurship and retail management.

After several months' negotiations with the Ghermezian brothers, a final decision was made in spring 1996 to move ahead with the project. The name for the mall has not been decided. For the moment it will be either Silver Spring Town Center or American Dream Mall, and the projected date of completion is 1998.

These megamalls are obviously exceptions. Very few more of them will be built. They are certainly not the wave of the future. But they represent the macro version of all malls and the human, if not American, penchant to have the biggest and the

best. Just as New York's World Trade Center had to outdo the
Empire State Building in height and both had to be outdone by
Chicago's Sears Tower, the Mall of America had to surpass the
size of Del Almo Mall in Torrance, California, now the second-
largest mall in the United States. "Build it and they will come"
seems to be the mantra of mall developers.

Traditional Religious Presence: Ministry to the Mall

MALL AREA RELIGIOUS COUNCIL

When plans were made to replace Metropolitan Stadium
with the Mall of America, several community religious leaders
convened to explore the relationship between their congrega-
tions and this huge commercial venture. What emerged from
these conversations was the formation in 1987 of the Mall Area
Religious Council (MARC), a group of over twenty-five religious organizations located in the vicinity of the Mall of America. They believed firmly that beyond the materialism of the
mall lie the spiritual values of generosity, personal dignity, com-
passion, and the unity of all people. Witness to these values
would be provided by MARC, a traditional, if nonsectarian, religious presence. It is not accidental that both James Rouse, a
practicing Christian, and the Ghermezians, an observant Jewish
family, emphasize the community tradition of each religion and
want to provide for a sense of human togetherness in their commercial enterprises. Jewish philosopher Martin Buber's famous
dictum "All real living is meeting" is not lost on Rouse or the
Ghermezians.[16]

The Reverend Delton Kreuger, president of MARC, has
sent me an abundance of material about the program. Kreuger
inaugurated MARC's presence in the mall by preaching at an
ecumenical service held in the rotunda and attended by about
five hundred people. From time to time there is discussion
about having services on a more regular basis, but as of now

✎ Pontius' Puddle

Copyright Joel Kauffmann

the mall management has prohibited them in public spaces. The fear is an old one; the aberrational and triumphalist aspects of religion could surface with disastrous consequences for all religious expression.

Chaplains from nearby Fairview Southdale Hospital (Lutheran), a member of MARC, may be called on to care for workers and shoppers who face human crises, such as illness, family problems, and drug use by youths. There is particular concern for the unexpected emergencies of out-of-state and international visitors.

In addition, MARC sponsored in December 1995 a very successful "holidays and holy days around the world" program that represented the rituals of several world religious traditions. It involved Buddhists, Jews, Muslims, Hindus, and representatives from several Christian denominations, all of whom welcomed visitors and provided the public with information about their respective sacred festivals. It was an ingenious way of bringing world religions to the mall, encouraging dialogue, and raising awareness of differences and similarities among religious communities.

A more or less permanent expression of this seasonal display is the Meaning Store, planned to open on November 1, 1997. Here, according to MARC's Home Page on the Internet, "visitors will have the opportunity to discover accurate information about world religious traditions, make contact with spiritual counseling services, and purchase literature, music and religious artifacts related to spiritual exploration." As Kreuger says, "The spiritual community brings to the public square a unique perspective on values and ethics. . . . The marketplace is where people, ideas, culture and commerce co-exist. MARC understands Creator God to be present in all aspects of daily life, including the Mall of America."

The work being done here by concerned ecumenical leaders is a model for what is eventually likely to appear in malls throughout the country. Maureen Hooley, public relations manager of the mall, welcomed MARC as a "credible broad-based religious organization."[17]

CHAPEL OF LOVE

The Chapel of Love, primarily reserved for weddings, is a strictly commercial enterprise developed by a local entrepreneur and sanctioned by the mall. It is unrelated to the Meaning Store and MARC. The Chapel fills a human need in a very effective commercial way. Brides and grooms buy and/or rent their gowns and tuxedos and other accessories in the mall bridal shops and then walk over to the Chapel for their wedding. Local judges, clergy, and other authorized persons officiate at these services. In fairness, some clergy boycott the Chapel because of the almost necessarily "secular" nature of the weddings performed there. But for many couples in the area without parish ties, it is the place of choice for their wedding.

Mall-Lingering

TEENS

The two human communities nurtured by EMACs (teens and seniors) have remained intact over the past decade, with more attention given to teens. They continue to come to the mall in droves. Their presence continues to be a rite of passage, perhaps more so than in the recent past.

It is now the common experience of American youths, the way farming was over a century ago, the trolley rides to school were for city children at the turn of the century, and high school was fifty years ago for all of us. Youths actually visit malls more consistently and more often than any other population. The mall remains their favorite hangout. A high school English teacher was spotted at the mall by his students. Their immediate response was, "What are you doing here? You're not a mall rat."

"Meet you at the mall." "Wanna go to the mall?" "Let's hang at the mall for a while." These are now ritual phrases among teenagers. Suburban humdrum takes them to the mall for diversion and excitement. Adolescents are congenitally social creatures, and personal interaction with peers can quickly alleviate boredom.

Parents find the mall a convenient, well-secured, and controlled environment — all ingredients for a relatively trustworthy child-sitter. It is a hermetically sealed island, moated by a parking lot and some distance from home. Once you are there, you will remain there. Teens have colonized the space. Older folks and serious shoppers, however, may find this youthful territoriality intimidating, and malls have taken steps to co-opt teens or to monitor with some seriousness their disruptive behavior.

Dufferin Mall of Toronto has dealt with an increasing teen presence by hiring its own youth counselor and setting aside a special space in the mall for teens only. After discussion among mall personnel staff, local high school principals, and the teens themselves, a "learning center" was created for classes, study rooms, and recreational activities. The program began in 1993 (a year when many malls in North America started such projects) not only to siphon off the energy that teens usually spend in making noise and blocking entrances, but also to effectively assist dropouts, potential dropouts, and somewhat committed high school students in enhancing their academic skills.

Again in 1993, Glendale Galleria in California initiated a "We Care . . . for Youth" program. It is really a job partnership for the mall and is designed for at-risk high school students. All services are free. It was such a successful program that Peter Ueberroth accepted it as part of his Rebuild LA, and it has been replicated in many communities in southern California.

Another attempt at dealing with the number of teens hanging out at the mall was the creation by Northgate Mall in San Rafael, California, of an interfaith community center in April 1993. It was the brainchild of local clergy and six local religious groups that saw the need for a place for teens to play games, to study, to surf the Internet with the computers provided, and, in general, to have fun. It operates from 3:00 P.M. to 9:00 P.M. and is always under adult supervision.

In 1994 the Mall of America opened an alternative high school, and a northern Virginia mall school, called Landmark Career Academy, was opened in Fairfax County. In the latter case there is vocational training, which accompanies traditional schoolwork. This means that the mall is more apt to be guaranteed better-qualified employees. Mall schools have the luxury of taking advantage of existing "cafeterias" as well as heating and air-conditioning systems — a considerable financial savings.

The push for malls to be more than a marketplace, and now to be more than a service and entertainment center, can be seen in the many and varied educational programs provided by churches, libraries, and schools. This makes the mall more of a complete human center than it was a decade ago. So instead of or in addition to being seen, looking for action, hanging out, or hooking up to go somewhere else, youths have more resourceful ways to spend their time in malls.

It is not lost on malls that teens also spend a good deal of money on tapes, food, video machines at the arcade, movies, and clothes. Malls initiate youths into our society's cult of materialism by seducing them into conspicuous consumption. Two generations removed from the Depression, mall rats in most cases have become what are called "cornucopia kids," young people who have been given too much. They have never wanted for anything, so the mall becomes their "wish-fulfilling tree."[18]

SENIORS

Seniors (fifty-five and over) are walking in the mall more routinely and in more sponsored programs. An observer remarked that they walk around the mall as if they own it. Well, they do! Their pension funds own about 276 malls nationwide, with about $7 billion invested in them!

Malls are replete daily with retirees, recovering cardiac patients, office workers, and mothers with strollers who walk around the mall. They come early, some at 7:00 A.M., before the shops open. Up to 89 percent of American EMACs allow free walking almost every day of the week.

Saturday morning at South Shore Mall in Bay Shore, Long Island, is filled with calorie-burning walkers, some walking 4 miles at a time. This Long Island mall, according to material provided by the International Council of Shopping Centers in New York, organized its walkers into "Club Tread," and the mall staff publishes a club news bulletin called "Treader Letter."

There has been, since 1988, the National Organization of Mall Walkers, and mall walkathons are becoming a big event for the Fairfield Mall in Chicopee, Massachusetts. These half-million mall walkers are not the zombies of *The Dawn of the Dead*. It's true that they like the climate-controlled comfort of the indoors, along with no bugs, heat, rain, mugging, barking and biting dogs (the inconveniences associated with walking outdoors). But on the whole these walkers are deeply in earnest, quite alert, and interesting people who desire to make their remaining years as healthy as possible.

Other groups have been formed to meet the needs and wants of the elderly. Prime Plus Club at Victoria Mall in Victoria, Texas, offers up to a 25 percent discount for purchases at participating stores. De Bartolo Malls in Florida have an annual Valentine's Day Heart Symposium in conjunction with the American Heart Association and the local hospital. At these events older folks can have cardiac risk factors, such as cholesterol and blood pressure, checked.

Mall managers know about the demographics of America's aging population. People over fifty-five account for 50 percent of spending and by 2020, nearly one-third of our population will be in this age bracket. There is a $900 billion market out there, according to the American Association of Retired Persons.

What primarily attracts seniors to the mall is not the mall but the company of their friends and companions. "It's like family here," said an Islip, Long Island, resident who covers 2 miles a day walking around the mall. There are camaraderie and a sense of needed community.

Of course, as a result of traipsing (walking twenty- to twenty-five-minute miles) by all the store windows in the mall, seniors are apt to spot an item that will bring them back after the shop opens. That is why, among other reasons, most malls will not permit jogging; you go past the windows too fast.

Mal de Mall

SAFETY

As I mentioned in the first edition, shopping malls have to hire security personnel, who walk a fine line between being public relations specialists and enforcers of mall regulations. Fear of crime is on the minds of most senior citizens, especially women, who do the bulk of our nation's shopping. So, naturally, concern for safety is a major issue for the mall.

The notion of the mall as a safe haven is eroding. In fact, the rate of crime in every category — shoplifting, shop holdups, auto break-ins and thefts, customer robberies, sex offenses, and assaults — has increased. Obviously, with the exception of shoplifting and the holdups, all the crime takes place in the parking lots or garages. Nevertheless, the mall is still one of the safest places to be in America. The raw number of crimes is quite small.

In response to actual criminal behavior and the perception of insecurity, malls have beefed up their security forces. Some malls, such as Tysons Corner in northern Virginia, have installed closed-circuit television cameras. Others have issued brochures to help customers ward off disaster; such brochures advise shoppers to park near well-lighted areas, put packages in the trunk of the car, have keys ready when they arrive at their cars, and shop with a partner. Police substations in some of our larger regional malls represent a more proactive mode.

Michael McGill, the loss-prevention director for Longs Drug Stores, reminds us that in an increasingly litigious society "the onus of crime prevention has fallen to store and mall operators, as people perceive that police agencies and the courts have failed to protect them." So malls have to walk that fine line between maintaining a low-profile presence of effective security and populating the mall with uniformed and armed security officers, which frighten customers. "You could," as McGill suggests, "end up with a shootout at the OK Corral over a tube of toothpaste."[19]

When the number of teens reaches critical mass and their behavior, especially excessive noise and the blocking of store entrances, has reached unacceptable levels, security is called. At the extreme, security personnel or police will ban the young perpetrators from the mall. For many teenagers, to be shunned by the mall and thereby isolated from their peers is a fate worse than death. This has proved to be an effective deterrent.

SHOPPING ADDICTION

If England was a nation of shopkeepers, we are surely a nation of shoppers. In an article entitled "Why Americans Love Their Malls," William Ecenbarger says, "Psychologists say shopping is an expression of power, a therapy for depression and guilt, and a cure for boredom, depression and loneliness. Shoppers are bombarded with opportunities to make themselves more lovable, comfortable, attractive, successful, powerful, healthy, intelligent and just plain happy."[20]

The shopping mall is a willing co-conspirator in our obsessive and compulsive urge to consume. For example, 93 percent of teenage girls rate shopping as their favorite activity. This cult of buying has even produced its own support groups and Twelve Step programs. Buying becomes a substitute for being loved. Slick promos, the creation of needs by Madison Avenue, TV commercials, the seduction of easy credit on Visa or Master-Card, and unrealistic expectations of what makes us happy all combine to place us in a precipitous free fall into an indebtedness that we cannot repay. Happiness is not at the end of a checkout line. Overconsumption, like tuberculosis, eventually takes our breath away.

Ironically, a Rouse mall, Santa Monica Place in Los Angeles, in an unhesitating act of self-criticism, sponsored an art exhibit last year that drew attention to the wastefulness of American consumerism. Robert Faulk, the mall's marketing manager, is quoted by *Baltimore Sun* reporter Liz Atwood as saying, "Shopping centers have a duty to offer not only goods, but ideas."[21]

THE MALL AND THE ENVIRONMENT

In addition to the malling of American landscapes mentioned in the first edition, malls are now being indicted for contributing heavily to the imbalance in our ecosystem. Soon after the Mall of America opened, Alan Thein Durning wrote a piece called "And Too Many Shoppers: What Malls and Materialism Are Doing to the Planet."[22] It is a searing critique of malls.

His thesis is that mall mania and its attendant consumerism not only are harmful to the environment but also provide no one with a sense of fulfillment. He further argues that our consumer lifestyle "erodes two key sources of a fulfilled life — family relationships and leisure time."

> America's thousands of shopping malls are the centerpieces of the most environmentally destructive ways of life yet devised. In combination, the suburbs that surround them, the cars that stream into them, the packaged throwaways that stream out of them, and the fast-food outlets and convenience franchises that mimic them cause more harm to the biosphere than anything else except perhaps rapid

population growth. . . . The mall-centered consumer lifestyle requires enormous and continuous inputs of the very commodities that are most damaging to the earth to produce: energy, chemicals, metals and papers. Americans consume close to their own weight in basic raw materials each day.

This critique is illustrated in the continuing clashes malls or mall-like structures have with environmentalists, historic preservationists, and county boards of supervisors. A case in point is the Disneyland clone planned for Manassas, Virginia, which would have been too close to Bull Run Battlefield. The new mall projected for Silver Spring, Maryland, is being held to an unprecedented amount of scrutiny by citizens' groups, and their prudence and caution will make for a healthier community.

CLASS

It would be difficult for malls not to reflect class consciousness, which is fast becoming the most determining social force in America, even more than race. As America becomes more classified, malls cannot be far behind.

The egalitarian, classless malls of James Rouse's vision (in which all ethnic and cultural groups would freely mingle) is still the predominant form, but it is not easily achieved. Housing patterns, changing demographics, corporate downsizing, and industry's mobility all tend to affect patronage of malls.

A striking case in point is the classist evolution of malls in the Baltimore metropolitan area. Golden Ring Mall, which was built in the vicinity of Bethlehem Steel Plant and Sparrows Point shipyards, naturally draws the blue-collar customer. White Marsh Mall, in suburban Baltimore, was for several years the upscale place to shop. In response to suburban gentrification, Owings Mills Town Center and Marley Station have become the higher-class malls, leaving White Marsh a solid, highly respected, middle-class mall.

There is a spectrum in the construction of these shopping centers from the garish and vulgar to the elegant and grand — from mass to class. Upscale communities, used to luxury retailing, will support a Galleria or a Tysons II with its prestige anchors, notwithstanding that some, such as Bloomingdale's and Saks Fifth Avenue, have come under hard times and have reached for their Chapter 11 bankruptcy escape hatches. In these malls there are a lot of marble, natural light, exclusive boutiques, and valet parking.

MALLAISE

Try as malls might, they lack the capacity to establish the organic *gemeinschaft* of primary communities such as Bel Air, the village square, and main street. In spite of their earnest efforts, there is always some dis-ease, some debility, a certain lack of health. Malls cannot finally overcome our anomie, our disorientation, isolation, anxiety, monotony, and boredom.

Malls are too airbrushed, antiseptic, sterile, artificial, homogenized, bland, plastic, and timeless to heal our brokenness. They are what William Kowinski calls "main street in a space ship." Malls always have to resist this charge not only from culture critics like Kowinski, but also from soccer leagues, quilters, local mom and pop convenience stores, and champions of ethnic diversity.

The following account was found in the August 1994 *Sports Illustrated*: "While strolling about the mall's four levels, I fall in behind two businessmen, one of whom produces a bleating cellular phone from his jacket. 'If it's for me,' says the other guy, 'tell them I'm not here.' In fact, no one is here, because here is . . . nowhere, a place of perpetual seventy-degree days and hospital cleanliness, a self-contained city that serves all needs, but one in which only Willis K. Carrier could feel comfortable."[23]

There is a good deal of truth in these comments on how malls fail us, but as much as malls are vilified by their despisers, for the past forty years they have served some significant human purpose beyond making a profit. Families, churches, and other primary groups will, it is to be hoped, continue to meet the needs of human community. But the fact remains that malls do mend some patches in our social garment. The possible pendulum to cybershopping does not appear to be a resourceful prospect, however. As one tourist said about West Edmonton Mall, "You can call this fake, but it's better than computers. At least here you have to deal with human beings face to face. Marketplaces never were meant to be places of intellectual debate."[24]

QUESTIONS

In addition to the foregoing criticisms, the future of malls as commercial and religious centers revolves around a genuine effort to face the following questions:

Are malls, through facelifts, renovations, and promotions, simply demonstrating a capacity to endlessly and creatively redefine themselves?

Are malls anachronistic at the turn of the millennium?

Do we have more than we need? Although there are some closings of malls, they reappear in phoenixlike fashion elsewhere.

Can a stagnant economy continue to support the relatively high retail and rental prices required by most malls? Will so-called cheaper power stores be an alternative — without the community and trappings that explicitly point to more than shopping?

Will our senses tire of the overload experienced at the mall?

Since profit is the bottom line, will not the invisible hand of the marketplace take care of the number and quality of malls?

What, if not the mall, is our alternative to human community and sacred centers?

Could we not have a "Hyde Park" corner in our large regional malls?

What will archaeologists think when, in five hundred years, they discover the shard remains of these commercial behemoths? Will they think that we were animated malls?

Mall Parks and Mall Ports

ORIOLE PARK AT CAMDEN YARDS

Soon after you present your ticket to an usher under the brick arches and pass through the iron gate, you find yourself on a pedestrian walkway that is the Eutaw Street corridor by the old warehouse at Camden Yards. You have entered a miniature Bourbon Street and carnival midway.

This concourse by the warehouse is what every good mall yearns for — a people place where food, camaraderie, and fun abide. Smoke rises from "Top this Dog," "Boog's Pit Beef," and "Bambino's Ribs." Customers carry draft beer on trays from a Maryland microbrewery. "Watch out for batted balls!" (Right field is only a few arm's lengths away.) "Programs here!" Across the midway from food concessions are the Oriole Baseball Store, the Camden Club, and the Baseball Galley, with every conceivable image and symbol of Oriole baseball history. There is the mandatory special section reserved for Cal Ripken, Jr., memorabilia.

People sit under canopied tables with folks they have not met before, and conversation easily flows by virtue of the breakdown of social distance created by a common interest in America's favorite pastime and the atmosphere evoked by the ballpark. You might also sit beneath an imposing bronze plaque that lists members of the Oriole Hall of Fame (a shrine within a shrine).

It is a human place; conviviality abounds, the hectic business pace in the high-rise office buildings a block away evaporates, the commuter ride is forgotten, and conversation is animated. Incidentally, a game is going on nearby with the Baltimore baseball pantheon in action, and the high god, Cal Ripken, Jr., is about to shatter Lou Gehrig's record of 2,030 continuous games played.

As you enter the ballpark proper, you are transported back in chronological time (it is 1912 in Fenway Park), even as you experience a qualitatively different space in the present (it is not the Charles Street business district or Baltimore row-houses). The atmosphere creates the mystery and power of Oriole Park, which has become a prototype of a space where baseball is played and the fan is free to celebrate the game. It is Baltimore's field of dreams and the reason for the deserved local and national attention. And the people sure have come.

What is the secret of this new $105.4 million structure with a 48,000-seat capacity? It began with the vision of Oriole President Larry Lucchino, who presided over negotiations and overall design under the tenure of successive owners Edward Bennett Williams and Eli Jacobs. RTKL, a Baltimore-based architectural and planning firm, was hired to create the master plan, which included the unique Eutaw Street corridor. Soon HOK, a Kansas City, Missouri, architectural firm, was engaged to design the entire complex at Camden Yards.

Lucchino then very wisely hired Janet Marie Smith, herself an accomplished architect, who became vice-president of stadium planning and development, a position she held from 1989 to 1994, at the Oriole organization. She and the Maryland Stadium Authority obtained the services of a bright and imaginative Baltimore graphic designer, David Ashton.

Smith was the voice of Lucchino and a key player in negotiations with HOK. Their relationship was a fortunate blend of advocacy and competence, and their product (Oriole Park) is a precedent-setting one. HOK was so successful in Baltimore that it was asked to design Jacobs Field in Cleveland and Coors Field in Denver. Smith, immediately and very gratefully, wants to credit the "talent at the table" (RTKL, HOK, and Ashton), without which the project would have failed.

It was then up to Smith and this team to creatively implement Lucchino's vision of an old-fashioned downtown park for no other sport than baseball, with an ambience of "traditional baseball values." It is now conventional wisdom that they surpassed all expectations.

They agreed that without a comfortable place for people to socialize, without a sense of human community, the baseball game and where it was played would be forgotten. They were committed to design a professional baseball field on a human scale, with a certain palpability that would be unmistakably felt throughout the entire park. It would even have an appeal for family members who don't care to watch the entire game. There would be a variety of food services, retail outlets, and entertainment activity.

It would be a BALLPARK, for baseball only, not an impersonal concrete cookie-cutter donut version of stadiums with off-putting fortresslike facades that are pockmarks on the urbanscape of America's cities. Furthermore, the latter often are used for several sports as well as concerts.

The desired warmth and human accessibility of Oriole Park are achieved by a regenerated look of the classic ballpark of almost a century ago. In an instructive foreword to Philip J. Lowry's recent book *Green Cathedrals,* Dale Swearingen, AIA, traces "three clearly defined stadium eras" of 20th-century baseball.[25] The first era was the classic ballpark — from Forbes Field in 1909 to Wrigley Field in 1914. In between were the Polo Grounds (1911), Fenway Park (1912), and Ebbetts Field (1913). The second era began in 1960 with the so-called super-stadium era or modernist era. It arrived with the likes of Candlestick Park (1960), the Astrodome (1965), Busch Stadium (1966), and Riverfront Stadium (1970).

Swearingen sums up the "overall failure" of the stadium era with a conversation he had with a fervent National League fan: "I watched the Cubs play from the upper deck of Wrigley Field and thoroughly enjoyed it, columns and all. I then watched the World Series from the upper deck of columnless Candlestick

Park and I couldn't see a thing without binoculars." The architects and fans of the 1990s have a nostalgia for the old ballparks, and there is a return to classic form with new building design.

Oriole Park at Camden Yards is Baltimore's attempt to regenerate the classic ballpark. This can be graphically portrayed in several ways.

Oriole Park is built on the site of the old Baltimore and Ohio Railroad yard near Camden Station in downtown Baltimore. This gives the park a contiguous relation to the city's famous Inner Harbor and allows downtown visually to enter the park by way of an open space between the scoreboard and the left field bleachers. The fan catches sight of church steeples, smokestacks, and rowhouses of "Bawlmer"; thus the park is organically connected to the life of the city, "a reference," according to Smith, "to what happens outside." Camden Yards serves as a park in the city; it is a neighborly space, and this is its genius.

Smith insisted on some central themes. It was to be an "old-fashioned ballpark with modern amenities." This meant the park would have nostalgia without being sentimental or saccharine, simplicity without being bland and homogenized, tradition without being cute (as in Disneyland); it would evoke the past without being regressive, reflect the game's history without becoming a dated period piece, remain grounded in the game without being held hostage to it.

Smith wanted desperately to avoid a theme park. She wanted a unique park with asymmetrical field dimensions and the timelessness of "crackerjack, Babe Ruth, and Ebbetts Field." She wanted a first-class park in looks and style, but as accessible as Main Street. As writer Edwin Warfield IV says, Oriole Park is "authentic without being pandering," and David Ashton comments, "It is a refreshing rebirth of the old."

This new old-fashioned park is a baseball village square, a return to the golden age of the game, when it was unashamedly our national pastime, when kids of every age delighted in going out to the ballpark. It is a harmonious blend of the bygone and the present, the kind of balance Smith planned.

What this means in practical terms is rich, natural grass on the playing field. It means intimate wraparound, low-down, close-to-the-action seating — not a threatening, vertigo-producing slope. You feel a part of the game. It means sweeping vistas without intruding columns to obstruct sight lines, all of which help spectators see the whole playing field and the electronic sign boards. It means brick and steel, not concrete Roman arches. It means an old-fashioned bleacher section. Janet Marie Smith succeeded in creating participatory space; you are in the park, and it is in you.

Smith's close partner was designer/artist David Ashton. His professional and personal metaphor is simplicity, a legacy of his Quaker background. Although "it *is* a gift to be simple," Ashton confesses that it is not easy! He brought that gift, however, to all the advertising he designed for the park and the signature signage for which he was completely responsible.

For example, the entrance sign, ORIOLE PARK AT CAMDEN YARDS, is composed of 3.5-foot-high stainless steel letters, not styrofoam, which was first suggested, and the scoreboard clock has hands, not digital numbers. In addition to these two most photographed symbols, he designed the logo based on a turn-of-the-century Oriole logo he retrieved from club archives. Furthermore, he created two Oriole Bird weather vanes; six orange pennants (three for the World Series won by the Birds and three for their division championships); clothing for the 183 ushers; a Coca-Cola sign with a *bottle*, not a can; and scrollwork around the ballpark clock.

Here is the least amount of anything plastic, synthetic, or artificial. Everything, thought Smith and Ashton, should complement the ballpark's purpose and history. Even the ads should tend toward that completeness and be a part of the architecture.

There is a new urban vocabulary at work here in this attempt to combine the past and present — illustrated in other ways by Los Angeles' Pershing Square and New York's Battery Park. Mark Hymn, *Baltimore Sun* writer, appreciates this new language as he writes about Oriole Park: "A sweeping brick architecture and erector set–like structured steel frame gives it the distinctive look of a ballpark that is well-connected, both to its downtown neighborhood and to baseball's past."[26]

And David Ashton, perhaps in unconscious religious (ritual and symbolic) language, describes the ballpark: "[Baseball] is not just hits and runs; it's the hot dogs, summer, grass, weathervanes, pennants. It's how you walk to your seat, the usher you get to know, the people that spill Coke on you. If that gets too controlled, it's lost."[27] The ballpark has become far more than a place where a game is played. Basketball and ice hockey are expected to follow suit.

PITTSBURGH INTERNATIONAL AIRPORT

Airports are not just for fliers anymore either! The 1990s have seen the international airport take on the form of the mall. Pittsburgh International Airport was the first to break out of the old mold and offer passengers and employees a wide range of shops, eateries, and services. It is the new paradigm for airports.

Finished in October 1992, the entire complex is accessible, with a large number of conveniences and services for the traveling person, whether it is for pleasure or business. Pittsburgh used the model provided by the British Airport Authority (BAA), now a private company, which operated shops at Heathrow and Gatwick and other U.K. airports. BAA encourages privatized business franchises as well as competitive prices so that a $0.59 small cup of coffee at McDonalds on the street is not $1.50 at the airport.

BAA is so serious about researching the buying habits of airline passengers that it knows what Japanese travelers like to take home and what exact whiskey Taiwanese prefer. Howard Banks, writing in *Forbes,* quotes a BAA retail director, Barry Gibson: "It's not rocket science, but unlike ordinary mall retailers, we know precisely who is going to be traveling where and when. And airport retail customers are mostly pretty well off."[28]

The new airport in Pittsburgh covers 13,000 acres, the third largest in the country after Denver and Dallas, and sees millions of passengers go through its gates annually. This is far more than a typical mall anchor store attracts. In fact, there is no need for the anchors required by malls because customers are already there. As they say, USAir is our best anchor, drawing 20 million a year.

There is a 60-foot-high ceiling in the main terminal room (the size of two football fields). Arches are there to remind us of the great Edwardian rail stations. There are lounges, markets, park benches, and trees, with the efficiency, amenities, and simplicity of the more successful malls. To be comfortable and functional is the goal.

The synergy between architecture and people is seen in the X-shape of the airport, which places every passenger as close as possible to the eight gates. This "hub" also prevents confusion and disorientation.

There are 10,000 square feet of leasable space for businesses. The many shops and restaurants target passengers who spend money while waiting for planes as well as the "meeters and greeters" who come to see them. This mall-like atmosphere is especially effective as a diversion for those there on layover and those who are preoccupied and anxious about their next flight. As with the typical nonairport mall, everything is here.

- Business services include fax machines, photocopiers, notary publics, traveler's checks, money orders, foreign money exchange, lost and found, and a U.S. Post Office.

- Kidsport, free to the public, consists of toys, books, and other activities for children; there are also a changing area for infants and a room for nursing mothers.

- Retail shops and restaurants, usually found at the mall, are present; these include TGIFriday, Steak and Plate, Chocolatiers, Ciro Jewelry, the Nature Company, the Body Shop, and Bon Voyage Travel Shop. The hook is that these national chains are required to charge for items at the airport the same prices that they charge at off-airport locations. The novelty about all this is that airport retailing now is far beyond the usual souvenirs, T-shirts, shot glasses, mugs, pennants, and bookstalls one finds in most airports.

- A reflection room, a nonsectarian chapel for moments of quiet and solitude, is present and serves the same purpose as the sectarian "Our Lady of the Skyways Chapel," which I visited at Logan International Airport in Boston in the late 1950s.

- An unusual aspect of Pittsburgh Airport is the $2 million in murals, sculptures, and "meditation gardens" a visitor finds there. This deserves special mention.

Art at the Mall

As Peter Morrin, the director of the J. B. Speed Museum in Louisville, Kentucky, has remarked: "Two sorts of people inhabit airports — the idle and blasé and the nervous and harassed. For both, the artworks come as a surprise and distraction, a relief from the tedious chain of events leading from departure to destination."[29] Art is so important for the Pittsburgh Airport that in the commemorative book published to celebrate its opening, an entire chapter by Jane A. Black is devoted to art. She notes that "instead of acquiring pieces of art to hang or sit about, the artwork was somehow to be woven into the very project." She notes how Joyce Pomeroy Schwartz, a consultant for the airport art committee from New York-based Works of Art for Public Spaces, wanted to challenge the artists to "put romance back into travel." "An airport," she says, "needs to be functional as well as 'welcoming, humane, people-oriented.'"[30] The airport has become more than a place for planes to land and take off.

So five artists, Jackie Ferrara, Maren Hassinger, Michael Morrill, Robert Morris, and Alan Saret, were commissioned to execute distinctive environmental art with an eye to facilitating ease of movement and enhancing the aesthetic experience of air travelers. Their needs would be uppermost in mind; the art would provide diversion, give direction, and extend comfort.[31]

Artist Ferrara created 70,000 square feet of floor space "with brightly colored (red, blue and gray) one-inch ceramic tiles to direct traffic and provide visual excitement," appropriately entitled *Paths*. According to the arts projects' brochure, "The design grew improvisationally, each section suggesting the next, and so on. Ferrara's inspiration was drawn from a science fiction story about a vast room with a curiously patterned floor; stepping on a certain sequence of tile, transported one into another dimension, in this case earth to sky."

Morris' work, *Steam Gardens,* the "signature piece" of the collection, is an exterior garden environment at the Landside Terminal on the baggage claim level next to the parking garage. It is a monumental minimalist sculpture (700 by 70 feet overall) functioning as five 7-foot-high teal-colored walled stone gardens, filled with steam, which forms and reforms shapes in the air, creating an atmosphere of contemplation for both travelers and airport employees.

Hassinger, a performance/video sculptor, created *Cloud Room* on the mezzanine level of the Airside core. It is a space where images of slowly drifting clouds are projected on the walls. This is a total environmental experience, with video, sound, seating, and flooring patterns simulating cloud formations, accompanied by natural sounds of crickets, birds, thunder, wind, rain, and the syncopation of beating drums. "A tranquil and comforting space," it is also known as the Reflection Room, a meditation place often used for religious services.

Morrill designed a "presentation of etched and sand-blasted colored glass panels for the international arm of the Airside building at the customs surveillance area, where it creates a see-through wall." The brochure describing the airport art tells us that these panels, "containing simple geometric patterns in various textures and hues, are not only aesthetically pleasing, but are also functional, as they can be closed to separate passengers who have been through passport security from the general public." His work is called *Compass*.

Saret, a Guggenheim award–winning sculptor, has created 55,000 square feet of computer-generated floor patterns in the transit and concourse areas of the Airside Terminal. Called *Home and Away,* this floor is a carefully considered pattern of tile squares, with recurring shades of blue to give the visitor a sense of scale between the "human" (the walkway) and the "immense" (the huge center rotunda). Saret really meant to organize the building with a color-coded pathfinding system to guide passengers to their right gate.

In addition to these works, Pittsburgh artist Peter Calaboyias has created *Silver Grid Wall,* a 68-foot-long bas relief sculpture made out of aluminum, and Akiko Kotani, born in Hawaii, has woven a 41-foot-long wall hanging of wool on linen. This tapestry represents the western Pennsylvania region and is appropriately called *Strip Mines.*

The upshot of all this and the overriding goal for Schwartz were an art concept that reflects on and informs us about the city of Pittsburgh, which has substantially reclaimed itself from industrial pollution. Completing the artistic airport picture were the restoration and return of Alexander Calder's master 600-pound mobile *Pittsburgh,* from the Carnegie Institute, where it had been for thirteen years, to the new Pittsburgh International Airport. This magnificent work is suspended in the skylight area of the airport above *Home and Away* and "transforms the central concourse level into an animated art-informed public mall experience." Here one can observe the delicate balance of the aluminum pieces and air currents of this well-known mobile.

Thomas H. O'Brien, chair and CEO of PNC Financial Corporation, states the obvious about the drastic changes taking place in airport construction in the 1990s. They are not for "commerce or tourism alone. . . . The new Pittsburgh International Airport will be a wonderful gateway for the arts. It will encourage others to come here to witness and participate in the rich cultural life of Pittsburgh. . . . And for our artists, the airport will represent easier travel to view the latest in the arts or start their own international tours."[32]

Nothing sums up the "more than" of the contemporary airport better than the guidebook to Pittsburgh International Airport. "Our goal is to offer the most pleasant and convenient airport in the world. We have attempted to combine the elegance of the great train stations of the nineteenth century with twenty-first century state-of-the-art technology. To soften the industrial nature of air transportation, works of art are built in, and the spacious rooms abound with natural light." Airports, like cathedrals and malls, have become patrons of the arts.

Just as Oriole Park is the prototype of future ballparks, Pittsburgh International Airport is the prototype of future airports. A case in point is the new Denver International Airport, completed in February 1995. A public relations video highlights the food, beverage, retail, service, and other concession tenants that occupy the mall-like space in the terminal and mezzanine and on the concourse.

The new Denver airport, however beleaguered, long delayed, and over budget, and notwithstanding the intense local controversy it has created, took great care in devising what it calls its "concessionaire program." There are over one hundred shops and restaurants, including a significant number of local businesses. They have done the usual marketing studies involving buying habits, average expenditure by customer, and number of passengers traveling through. While a majority of concessions provide food items, over 40 percent of the shops carry newspapers, gifts, books, and boutique stands. There are also the necessary ATMs, as well as a game room with pool tables. A chiropractor has an office for those who need a pre-flight alignment. In addition to all this, there is the expected duty-free shop found in all international ports.

The innovating aspect of the Denver International Airport concessionaire program is the attention given to minority-owned business enterprises and the encouragement the airport has given them to set up shop there. This includes reasonable rent and a street pricing policy. To the astonishment of everyone, the air mall took in $1.6 million the first six days of business. In its first year, it was cited as the top mall in the Colorado area.

Airport spokespersons intentionally use the word "mall" when referring to their large number of concessions. Passengers are told that what they will experience at Denver is just what they experience in their local mall. "It's like shopping in a mall," they are told. This appears to be an attempt to convey the continuity between the habits of off-airport shoppers and those who patronize the airport mall.

The mall orientation of major airports has found its way to Baltimore-Washington International Airport (BWI). Merchandise sales alone are expected to be $6 million for the fledgling BWI mall in 1995 (some fifty shops). This is far more than predicted and presages a retail boom for an airport not intended to be a mall. According to Suzanne Wooton, *Baltimore Sun* staff writer, "by early next year [1996], the airport will add a third Starbucks — at the end of Pier D, which is used largely by USAir commuter traffic, and a natural fruits and nuts store known as the Grove and possibly a compact disc and tape shop."[33] In most cases, these items are priced at street levels, not the usual premium ones typical of airport kiosks and shops. Finding available commercial space for retailers is becoming more and more difficult as BWI enters this competitive world initiated by Pittsburgh International Airport. According to Wooton, this trend at airports will continue nationwide "to accommodate harried travelers who often have more money than time."

A unique bit of art graces the open space near the departing gate of BWI. David Ashton, of Oriole Park fame, designed 150 geese in flight. They are made of corten steel and staked to the ground of a 500-foot-long spectacular garden to represent (again that simplicity) the fact that Baltimore and the Chesapeake Bay are flyways for Canadian geese. Each steel goose weighs 28 pounds and has a wingspan of 5 to 6 feet. The whole flock is positioned in such a way to form an "undulating ribbon" from 5 to 10 feet above the garden.

Edward Gunts, in a *Baltimore Sun* article, says, "Designed as a unifying element for the garden, the steel geese will make a metaphorical link between the airport and region it serves."[34] The garden, called "Seasons in Flight," is meant to be a gateway to the Maryland and District of Columbia areas. The ornamental grass and local flora evoke the tidewater of Maryland. No one will think he or she is in the Southwest. What more appropriate sculpture is there for meeters and greeters to see as they leave the airport!

Just as a tourist can fly around the world and by virtue of staying in Hilton hotels at every stop never leave America, airline passengers will soon be able to fly throughout the United States and never leave a mall. Architecture, art, and environment are symbiotically related as the "outside" is brought in — Baltimore City comes into Oriole Park; the Chesapeake Bay, by way of Ashton's geese, comes into Baltimore-Washington International Airport; Pittsburgh enters its airport by way of uniquely designed works of art. Where is the line between us and the mall?

Myth of the Mall: Malls 'R' Us

"I believe in the mall of America and the center of life it has become, one shopping experience providing personal and material pleasure for all." Just as the Pledge of Allegiance does not represent liberty and justice for all, only some liberty and justice for all and liberty and justice for some, the mall does not represent to all what the foregoing creed suggests. But there is a sufficient number of people experiencing the "beyond" of the marketplace in malls that religious scholars can unashamedly take this anagogic experience and cultural phenomenon seriously. Furthermore, in the concluding paragraph of a brilliant review of Ronald Grimes' *Symbol and Conquest: Public Ritual and Drama in Santa Fe,* Davíd Carrasco indirectly reinforces the religious nature of malls by this observation: "The notion that public nonliterary symbols in a contemporary American city constitute valuable texts for the study of religion is intelligently represented."[35] Although Carrasco is referring to the "symbol system of Santa Fe's public religion," and its "union of *ecclesia* and *civitas,*" it is more than an oblique reference to the importance of contemporary shopping malls ("nonliterary symbols") as "valuable texts for the study of religion."

I understand myth to be an untrue story (without denying a historical basis) that points to a truth about human community and the activities of the gods. A myth is to be looked through, not at, to the reality to which it points and that it describes. What I have been trying to say about the religious character of malls can be summarized best by spelling out the mythical nature of the mall as a center.

The mall "story" is so pervasive and has so captured the imagination of our communities that in many cases the latter's meaning and significance are established with reference to the mall. The story (myth) of the mall is created by the community and reflects the truth about the human condition of that community — its underlying values and meanings. What do we see when we look "through" and "beyond" the mall?

PILGRIMAGE CENTER

The Mall of America draws more visitors and tourists than the Vatican and Mecca, while it is topped in this country only by Disney World and country music center of Branson, Missouri. (One-half of all visitors to the Mall of America are either foreign or domestic tourists.) The inclusion in some of the larger malls of 1,000-room hotels and extravagant entertainment complexes reinforces the notion of pilgrimage and shrine.

In November and December, Christmas shoppers use Northwest Airlines for one-day package deals from the District of Columbia to the Twin Cities. They leave early in the morning and return to the nation's capital very late the same day. In between, as they enter the mall's colorful display and multilayered lushness, they probably feel overwhelmed and awed by it all. There is that pilgrim sense of expectancy accompanying arrival and entry into the shrine.

Malls, more and more, see themselves as objects of, or a station along, vacation routes. West Edmonton's Fantasyland regularly attracts thousands of tourists, visitors, and shoppers from a 300-mile radius, whereas the traditional regional mall pulls people from a 10- to 15-mile radius. Many drive from three western Canadian provinces, and there are shuttle flights eleven times a week to West Edmonton from Toronto, St. Paul, Seattle, and Vancouver. These flights are usually for three days at the mall and two nights in the mall hotel.

The King of Prussia Mall, near Philadelphia, the largest mall on the East Coast, is usually part of tour packages created by the nearby Valley Forge convention and visitors bureau. Admittedly, the megamall is more of a tourist attraction, but all malls, to a degree, become a pilgrim center in the usual understanding of the word in religious studies.

Pilgrimage means *separation* from familiar surroundings as the adventure begins. *Liminality* ensues as the journey continues and the shrine is visited. *Ordeal* is associated with liminality; what better example is there than being lost in a sea of cars in the mall parking lot or finding the proper exit from the mall to your space in that lot? Finally, there is *reincorporation* into the former community not as a new person, but as one with a new and treasured experience. Can you imagine the tales told by these 20 million visitors as they journey to and from their homes? After all, they are pilgrims, not crusaders; they are about play, not work.

CEREMONIAL CENTER

Malls continue, in more ways than ever, to follow a calendrical cycle and to celebrate seasonal events reflecting national, religious, and business holidays and holy days. This ritual activity helps us participate in the myth of the mall.

The *national* celebrations of July 4, Presidents' Day, and Thanksgiving are duly acknowledged. Corridors and storefronts are bedecked with Old Glory's red, white, and blue. Malls are nothing if not patriotic.

Of all the *religious* holy days, Christmas and Hanukkah stand out well beyond second-place Easter and Passover. Decorations, local choirs, ornate displays, Santa, and the Easter Bunny are capstones of those ritual times. Almost all this ceremonial life occurs at the mall's hub, under the atrium, by the large pool — its geographical and human center.

Business promotions, such as sidewalk sales, spring sale days, and back-to-school days, continue to punctuate the slow times in between the bigger holiday crunches. They also exploit the family and personal celebrations of Valentine's Day, Mother's Day, Father's Day, Grandparent's Day, and Secretary's Day. Somewhere in the midst of all this is some form of Halloween during October.

The mall's yearly round, with its liturgical regularity and ritual clarity, synchronizes well with the individual and social celebrations of many of the patrons who support the mall. This symbiotic relationship will have to continue in order for the mall to exist.

FESTIVAL CENTER

Tourists, visitors, and shoppers are expected to have fun at the mall, to play, to enjoy shopping, to be entertained. Most of it is free; some have a price tag (movies and video games).

The Rouse Company pioneered the festival marketplace, now continued on a bigger scale by the Ghermezian brothers with Camp Snoopy and Fantasyland. But many smaller malls usually have clowns, mimes, magicians, tumblers, jugglers, roving minstrels, ice-skating rinks, carousels, twelve-screen movie theaters, and video arcades, topped off with food courts and eateries to satisfy the most fastidious of palates.

The mall, from this point of view, is an amusement park and social event surrounded by shops. Recreation amid retailing seems the cutting edge of successful malls.

In June 1995 the Broadway Mall of Hicksville, Long Island, advertised in *This Month on Long Island* that "shopping here is a really fun event." This was being said fifteen years ago by malls from California to Florida to Texas.

HUMAN SERVICE CENTER

As I mentioned in the earlier part of the book, the designation of a space as "center" almost always conveys the message that significant human interaction or the desire to supply human need takes place here. My first edition documented this trend of malls to concentrate their efforts on noncommercial activity and self-consciously to become service providers. This trend has increased with the number of medical, dental, and counseling practitioners available in addition to reproductive health clinics and mobile immunization units. Financial and professional needs are met by ATMs, fax machines, copiers, the usual banking services, and the federal post office.

The cultural dimension is not omitted. Museums, art galleries, schools, interfaith religious activities, and library branches are currently found in malls. Elementary school children often take field trips to malls when the latter provide certain historical, scientific, and other educational exhibits.

The catholicity (universality) of these centers is further illustrated in the opportunity "to meet your politician at the mall," and to sponsor checker tournaments and cheerleading contests. United Way launches its annual drive from malls, and softball and soccer league participants register there.

SYMBOLIC CENTER

Mall architecture unmistakably re-creates the center by use of colossal crosses, squares, and circles — an axis mundi. This integrating form directs human movement and attempts to give the visitor a sense of stability, unity, and meaning. The physical nature of the center's quadrilateral structure reminds the shopper of psychical centeredness.

It is not an accident that large public spaces — from cathedrals, to the University of Chicago campus, to most malls — carefully inform us that, by way of aisles, walkways, gates, and arches, all paths lead to the center. We seem always in procession, on parade, or watching the promenade and all the while being directed to the center. It is a kind of choreography, a theatrical production with actors, audience, stage props, all of which are really a set for a "communal social life."[36] This propensity to center is seen also in the new Pittsburgh International Airport, with its distinct hub.

The mall has become a "ritual-architectural event," to use Lindsay Jones' phrase. There is a dialectical relation between the "architecture itself, human users, and ceremonial occasions that bring people and architecture together in a 'to and fro involvement.' "[37] So at the center are ceremonial activity, ritual behavior, meals, play, and community. All of this tends to happen only at the center, or as Eliade and Lawrence Sullivan say in their *Encyclopedia of Religion* article on the nature of the center:

> The symbolism of the center, with great consistency of meaning, applies to the center of the universe, the center of the residential unity, the center of the village, the home, the ritual space, the human physiology mystically conceived, and art of spiritual concentration. On every plane, the significance of the symbol of the center of the world underlies the fact that at the heart of existence lies an experience and mode of being entirely different from the ordinary world centered on it.[38]

Perhaps architectural critic Robert Campbell is right. Our generation's "mythic building" is the mall, "where, mysteriously, for a time, the Delphic air vibrates."[39]

Acknowledgments

For the writing of this chapter, I am indebted to the following persons:

Mike Tubridy, of the International Council of Shopping Centers, New York, for helpful statistics about the number and growth of malls.

Janet Marie Smith, Director of Planning and Development, Atlanta Braves, for her insight into the overall planning of Oriole Park at Camden Yards in Baltimore, and graphic designer David Ashton, of Baltimore, for the interpretation of his many designs, which help give Oriole Park its special character.

My colleagues Dr. Gregory Alles, Chair of the Philosophy and Religious Studies Department at Western Maryland College, and Dr. Davíd Carrasco of Princeton University's Religion Department, for their helpful comments and criticisms. I cannot thank them enough. They are plumbing depths whose surfaces I'm just now scratching.

The Office of Marketing/Governmental Affairs, Denver International Airport, for a promotional video about its "mall."

Joyce Muller, Office of Public Information at Western Maryland College, for proofreading of this chapter and for her support, which knows no bounds.

Dorothy Shindle, who typed the first manuscript ten years ago and who, in her own efficient way, agreed to put this chapter in presentable order.

Hugh G. Hachmeister, AIA, Principal Architect, Pittsburgh International Airport, for his extremely helpful information about the public art in that airport.

Jody Berman, of the University Press of Colorado, for her unusual forbearance and wise guidance.

Delton Kreuger, President of Mall Area Religious Council at the Mall of America, for assistance in understanding the ecumenically religious program he coordinates there.

Notes

Chapter 1 More than a Marketplace:

The Religious Nature of Shopping Malls

1. The Baltimore Sunday *Sun*, December 12, 1982.
2. *U.S. News and World Report*, June 18, 1973, p. 43.
3. Eliade, Mircea, *Cosmos and History: The Myth of the Eternal Return*. Trans. by Willard R. Trask, New York: Harper and Row Torchbook, 1959, p. 4.

Chapter 3 The Shopping Mall as Sacred Space

1. Tuan, Yi-Fu, *Space and Place: The Perspective of Experience*, Minneapolis: University of Minnesota Press, 1977, p. 88.
2. Wheatley, Paul, *The Pivot of the Four Quarters*, Chicago: Aldine Publishing Co., 1972, p. 434.
3. *Ibid.*, p. 68.
4. Eliade, Mircea, *Cosmos and History: The Myth of the Eternal Return*, p. 10.
5. Tuan, p. 88.
6. Wheatley, p. 53.
7. Eliade, p. 28.
8. Quoted in Wheatley, p. 57.
9. Eliade, Mircea, *Images and Symbols: Studies in Religious Symbolism*, New York: Sheed and Ward, 1969, p. 52.
10. Eliade, p. 12.
11. Pettigrew, Jim, Jr., "The Waterfront Revivals," *Sky*, January, 1984, p. 52.
12. Rouse, James, Unpublished speech "The Philadelphia Story," pp. 8–9.
13. Asimov, Isaac, "Life in the 21st Century," *Modern Maturity*, Feb.–Mar., 1984, p. 38.
14. Naisbitt, John, *Megatrends: Ten Directions Transforming Our Lives*, New York: Warner Communications Co., 1984, p. 35.

Transition James Rouse — Mahatma of Malls

1. Rouse, James, Unpublished speech "Places That Make a Difference," pp. 3–4.
2. Cauthen, Kenneth, *The Ethics of Enjoyment*, Atlanta: John Knox, 1975, p. 64.

3. Rouse, James, Unpublished speech "The Transformation of the City: A Forecast," p. 18.
4. Rouse, James, Unpublished speech "Utopia: Limited or Unlimited," p. 2.
5. *Ibid.*
6. Rouse, James, Unpublished speech "Make No Little Plans," p. 29.
7. Rouse, James, Unpublished speech "It Can Happen Here," p. 3.
8. *U.S. News and World Report*, June 18, 1973, p. 46.

Chapter 4 Mall as Sacred Time

1. Huizinga, Johan, *Homo Ludens: A Study of the Play Element in Culture*, Boston: Beacon Press, 1966, p. 132.
2. Cherlin, Merrill, "The Allure of Shopping," *Baltimore Sun Magazine*, April 8, 1984, p. 25.
3. Rouse, James, "The Philadelphia Story," p. 9.
4. Caillois, Roger, *Man, Play, and Games*, New York: Free Press, 1961, p. 23.
5. Miller, David, *Gods and Games: Toward a Theology of Play*, New York: Harper and Row, 1970, p. 176.
6. Wheatley, Paul, *The Pivot of Four Quarters*, p. 418.
7. Campbell, Robert, "Evaluation: Boston's 'Upper of Urbanity': Faneuil Hall Marketplace After Five Years," *AIA Journal*, June, 1981, p. 26.
8. Rouse, James, Unpublished speech "The New Marketplace," p. 2.
9. Canty, Donald, "Baltimore's Lively Downtown Lagoon," *AIA Journal*, June, 1981, p. 34.
10. Keen, Sam, *The Passionate Life*, New York: Harper and Row Publishers, 1983, p. 99.
11. Tillich, Paul, *The Protestant Era*, Abridged Edition, Trans. by James Luther Adams, Chicago: University of Chicago Press, 1957, p. 117.

Chapter 5 Concluding Observations: From Lenox Square to Bel Air

1. Rouse, James, Unpublished Speech, "Make No Little Plans," p. 19.
2. Butler, Patrick, "Mall Adjusted," *Saturday Review*, June 20, 1970, p. 6. The artificial nature of the EMAC — its antiseptic and virtually self-contained world — may provide a prototype of future space colonies. Colonies in space may not look very different from some of our large regional malls. Indeed, in his recent book, Gerald K. O'Neill, a Princeton physics professor, states that humans will be able to build "hollow worlds in space, with sunshine, atmosphere, and earthlike environment, and the equivalent of gravity produced by rotation." *Harvard Magazine*, March/April, 1979, p. 45.

Chapter 6 The Mall Is Not Over

1. Lambert, Craig, "Space and Spirit," *Harvard Magazine*, March/April 1995, p. 34.
2. Kowinski, William, "Endless Summer at the World's Biggest Shopping Wonderland," *Smithsonian,* December 1986, p. 42.
3. See Smith, Jonathan Z., *Drudgery Divine,* Chicago: University of Chicago Press, 1990, esp. Chapter 1; and Smith, Jonathan Z., *Map Is Not Territory*, Leiden: E. J. Brill, 1978, in which Smith criticizes Eliade's notion of the symbol of the center. This criticism continues at some length in Smith, Jonathan Z., *To Take Place*, Chicago: University of Chicago Press, 1987. See also two helpful articles by Gregory Alles: "Surface, Space, and Intention: The Parthenon and the Kandariya Mahadeva," *History of Religions* 28, 1 (August 1988), pp. 1–37, and "Wach, Eliade, and the Critique from Totality," *Numen* 35, 1 (1988), pp. 108–138.
4. Cited in Cave, David, *Mircea Eliade's Vision for a New Humanism,* Oxford: Oxford University Press, 1993, p. 18. Incidentally, Cave finds "morphology" a more flexible and useful term than "patterns."
5. Ibid., p. 196.
6. See Reisman, David, *The Lonely Crowd,* New Haven: Yale University Press, 1973. Robert Bellah et al. have restated the tension between individualism and community in American life in *Habits of the Heart,* Berkeley: University of California Press, 1985.
7. *Baltimore Sun,* January 1, 1994.
8. It is interesting to note that Albert Mehrabian in *Public Places and Private Spaces,* New York: Basic Books, 1976, pp. 205–297, devotes the part of his book called "Play Environments" to the various ways public spaces are utilized. This appreciable part of the book contains eight individual chapters dealing with movies, theater, museums and galleries, libraries, bars and restaurants, sports arenas, stores, and travel (vacation). Now all of these can be found under one roof in many malls.
9. Quoted in Apgar, Sally, "Japanese Hope to Top U.S. Megamalls," *Carroll County Times* (Westminster, Md.), January 17, 1993.
10. Lukas, Jeanne Marie, "Of Mice and Malls," *U.S. News and World Report,* September 10, 1995, p. 7.
11. Fisher, Marc, "Where Hunters Gather," *Washington Post Magazine,* September 3, 1995, p. 32.

12. Anderson, Jon, "Monster Mall," *Chicago Tribune,* January 18, 1987. The first quote is from Bernie Brown, a Chicagoan who was visiting the mall for the first time, and the second is from Anderson himself.
13. Kowinski, William, "Endless Summer at the World's Biggest Shopping Wonderland," *Smithsonian Magazine,* December 1986, p. 41.
14. Ibid., p. 37.
15. Quoted in Aguilar, Louis, "Developers to Cut Size of Mall Complex," *Washington Post,* October 29, 1995. "As of November, 1996, the state of Maryland and the Ghermezian brothers are negotiating the appropriate share of public and private funding for the mall. *Baltimore Sun* editorial, November 14, 1996 pg. 18A. The project is technically on hold as the book goes to print.
16. Buber, Martin, *I and Thou,* Edinburgh: T. and T. Clark, 1953, p. 13.
17. Hooley, Maureen, "At Mall of America, Ministry Will Reach Out to Workers, Visitors," *Baltimore Sun,* August 22, 1992.
18. It is only fair to mention that a small number of teens from Cleveland Heights, Ohio, to New York City, to Costa Mesa, California, are protesting the present makeup of malls. They dislike the number of older people there, the codes of conduct that malls have directed at youth, and the sameness of so many suburban malls. "Malls are just air-conditioned boxes that suck people in," said one teenager who helped develop the antimall called The Lab in Costa Mesa. From "Malls Are Now Totally Uncool, Say Hip Teens," *Carroll County Times,* May 9, 1996, p. 1G. "It remains to be seen whether this movement will provide an adequate substitute for the "malling around:" currently enjoyed by many teens." I suggested this sentence in my response to Ms. Lionheart, September 5, 1996, item #7.
19. Quoted in Cockerham, Paul W., "Safe Shopping," *Stores,* June, 1994.
20. Ecenbarger, William, "Why Americans Love Their Malls," *Philadelphia Inquirer Magazine*, September 1, 1985, p. 12.
21. Atwood, Liz, "Malls Are Changing into Entertainment Centers," Baltimore Sun, October 30, 1995.
22. Durning, Alan Thein, "And Too Many Shoppers: What Malls and Materialism Are Doing to the Planet," *Washington Post,*

August 24, 1992, p. 3C. "Other critics of the materialism of malls are James Wallis' *Soul of Politics: Beyond 'Religious Right and Secular Left.'* New York: Harcourt Brace and Co., 1995. See especially Chapter 7, "I Shop, Therfore I am," pp. 150–172 and Robert C. Robert, "Just a Little Bit More: Greed and the Malling of our Souls," *Christianity Today*, April 8, 1996, pg. 30–33.

23. Rushin, Steve, "1954–1994: How We Got Here," *Sports Illustrated*, August 1994, p. 64.

24. Aguilar, Louis, "Montgomery Reviewers Find Humongous Mall Is a Hit with Canadians," *Washington Post*, October 22, 1995.

25. Swearingen, Dale, "Foreword," in Lowry, Philip J., *Green Cathedrals*, New York: Addison-Wesley Publishing Co., 1992.

26. Hymn, Mark, "Here's the Ticket: A Fan's Guide," *Baltimore Sun*, March 29, 1992, p. 3M.

27. Quoted in Shapiro, Stephanie, "O's and the Arts," *Baltimore Sun*, April 3, 1992, p. 3F.

28. Gibson, Barry, "Tomorrow, the World: The BAA Spreads Its Wings Beyond the UK," *Forbes*, December 18, 1996, p. 178.

29. Quoted in "The New Pittsburgh International Airport Public Art Project." This is a brochure distributed by the airport's Public Information Office. Washington National Airport in the nation's capital has embarked on a serious program of public artworks. See Reid, Alice, "Art to Take Airport to New Heights," *Washington Post*, August 1, 1996, pp. 1, 8MD.

30. Tascarella, Patty, ed., *Pittsburgh International Airport: A Commemorative Edition*, 1992, p. 42.

31. I am further indebted to Hugh G. Hachmeister, AIA, principal architect of Pittsburgh International Airport, for invaluable information about the artwork there. It is found in a booklet entitled "The New Pittsburgh International Airport Public Art Projects."

32. Tascarella, ed., *Pittsburgh International Airport*, p. 74.

33. Wooton, Suzanne, "At BWI, a Touch of the Mall," *Baltimore Sun*, December 2, 1995.

34. Quoted in "Symbolic Flight: 150 Geese Will Hover at BWI," *Baltimore Sun,* December 16, 1993.

35. Carrasco, Davíd, "The Conqueror and His Virgin," *History of Religions* 18, no. 3, February 1979,. p. 284.
36. Lennard, Suzanne, and Henry Lennard, *Public Life in Urban Places*, Southampton, N.Y.: Gondolier Press, 1984, pp. 21, 37.
37. Jones, Lindsay, *Twin City Tales: A Hermeneutical Reassessment of Tula and Chichén Itzá*, Niwot, Colo.: University Press of Colorado, 1995, p. 186.
38. Eliade, Mircea, and Lawrence, Sullivan, "Center of the World," *Encyclopedia of Religion*, vol. 3, p. 171.
39. Campbell, Robert, "Evaluation: Boston's 'Upper of Urbanity' Faneuil Hall Marketplace After Five Years," *AIA Journal,* June 1981.

Selected Bibliography

BOOKS

Caillois, Roger. *Man, Play, and Games*. New York: Free Press, 1961.

Cauthen, Kenneth. *The Ethics of Enjoyment*. Atlanta: John Knox, 1975.

Eliade, Mircea. *Cosmos and History: The Myth of the Eternal Return*. Trans. Willard Trask. New York: Harper and Row, 1959.

―――. *Images and Symbols: Studies in Religious Symbolism*. New York: Sheed and Ward, 1969.

―――. *Patterns of Comparative Religion*. Trans. Rosemary Sheed. New York: World Publishing, 1963.

―――. *The Sacred and the Profane*. Trans. Willard R. Trask. New York: World Publishing, 1959.

Huizinga, Johan. *Homo Ludens: A Study of the Play Element in Culture*. Boston: Beacon Press, 1966.

Jacobs, Jerry. *The Mall*. Prospect Heights, Ill.: Waveland Press, 1985.

Jones, Lindsay. *Twin City Tales: A Hermeneutical Reassessment of Tula and Chichén Itzá*. Niwot, Colo.: University Press of Colorado, 1995.

Kowinski, William Severine. *The Malling of America*. New York: William Morrow, 1985.

Lennard, Suzanne J. Crowhurst, and Henry L. Lennard. *Public Life in Urban Places*. Southhampton, N.Y.: Gondolier Press, 1984.

Lowry, Philip J. *Green Cathedrals: The Ultimate Celebration of All 273 Major League and Negro League Ballparks*. New York: Addison-Wesley, 1992.

Marx, Leo. *Machine in the Garden*. New York: Oxford University Press, 1964.

Mehrabian, Albert. *Public Places and Private Spaces: The Psychology of Work, Play, and Living Environments.* New York: Basic Books, 1976.

Miller, David. *Gods and Games: Toward a Theology of Play.* New York: Harper and Row, 1970.

Mumford, Lewis. *The City in History.* New York: Harcourt Brace and World, 1961.

Naisbett, John. *Megatrends: Ten New Directions Transforming Our Lives.* New York: Warner Communications, 1984.

Tuan, Yi-Fu. *Space and Place: The Perspective of Experience.* Minneapolis: University of Minnesota Press, 1977.

Venture, Robert, Denise Scott Brown, and Steven Izenour. *Learning from Las Vegas: The Forgotten Symbolism of Architectural Form.* Rev. ed. Cambridge, Mass.: MIT Press, 1994.

Walter, Eugene Victor. *Placeways: A Theory of the Human Environment.* Chapel Hill: University of North Carolina Press, 1988.

Wheatley, Paul. *The Pivot of the Four Quarters.* Chicago: Aldine, 1971.

———. "The Suspended Pelt: Reflections on a Discarded Model of Spatial Structure." In *Geographic Humanism, Analysis, and Social Action,* ed. Donald S. Deakins et al. Ann Arbor: University of Michigan, 1977, pp. 147–148.

ARTICLES

Advertising Supplement. "More at the Mall: Malls and Centers—the New Main Street." *Washington Post Magazine,* November 26, 1989, pp. 1–11.

Anderson, William R., and Herbert Sprouse. "Museums in the Marketplace." *Museum News* (October, 1984), pp. 59–67.

Breckenfeld, Gurney. "The Rouse Show Goes National." *Fortune,* July 27, 1981, pp. 49–54.

Campbell, Robert. "Evaluation: Boston's 'Upper of Urbanity' Faneuil Hall Marketplace After Five Years." *AIA Journal* (June 1981), pp. 24–31.

Canty, Donald. "Baltimore's Lively Downtown Lagoon." *AIA Journal* (June 1981), pp. 33–41.

Coyne, Patrick. "Oriole Park at Camden Yards." *Communication Arts* (September/October, 1992), pp. 102–107.

Demarest, Michael. "He Digs Downtown." *Time,* August 24, 1981, pp. 42–49.

Ecenbarger, William. "Why Americans Love Their Malls." *Philadelphia Inquirer Magazine*, September 1, 1985, pp. 10–17.

Finkel, David. "The Malling of Silver Spring: The Ghermezians and the American Dream." *Washington Post Magazine*, December 10, 1995, pp. 16–21, 30–36.

Kowinski, William. "Endless Summer at the World's Biggest Shopping Wonderland." *Smithsonian* (December 1986), pp. 35–43.

———. "The Malling of America." *New Times,* May 1, 1978, pp. 32–55.

Lambert, Craig. "Space and Spirit." *Harvard Magazine* (March/April, 1995), pp. 34–41.

Palmer, Barbara. "Dollars and Dreams: The Jim Rouse Story." *Baltimore Magazine* (May 1979), pp. 75–79, 138–148.

Rushin, Steve. "It's All in the Mall." *Sports Illustrated*, August 16, 1994, pp. 63–66.

Thompson, Ricki. "Attracted and Repelled by the Mall of America." *Sojourners* (September/October 1993), pp. 18–20.

UNPUBLISHED SPEECHES BY JAMES ROUSE

"The National Shopping Center: Its Role in the Community It Serves." Seventh Annual Design Conference, Harvard, April 26, 1963.

"It Can Happen Here." Conference on Metropolitan Future, University of California, Berkeley, September 23, 1963.

"Make No Little Plans." International New Towns Association Conference, Barcelona, Spain, October 3, 1983.

"The New American Marketplace: A Challenge to Department Store Leadership." Annual Meeting of Associated Merchandising Corporation, The Greenbrier, April 27, 1976.

"The Philadelphia Story." Annual Meeting of American Merchandising Corporation, The Greenbrier, May 3, 1978.

"Places That Make a Difference." Remarks to shareholders of the Rouse Company at its annual meeting, May 23, 1979, on the occasion of its fortieth anniversary and his retirement as chief executive officer.

"The Transformations of the City—a Forecast." National Retail Merchants Association, Scottsdale, Arizona, February 7, 1979.

"Utopia: Limited or Unlimited." National Housing Conference, New York, November 14–16, 1979.

Index